W9-AFI-485

Social Issues in Literature

Women's Issues in Nathaniel Hawthorne's *The Scarlet Letter*

Other Books in the Social Issues in Literature Series:

Class Conflict in F. Scott Fitzgerald's *The Great Gatsby*

Depression in J.D. Salinger's *The Catcher in the Rye*

Industrialism in John Steinbeck's *The Grapes of Wrath*

Issues of Class in Jane Austen's *Pride and Prejudice*

Male/Female Roles in Ernest Hemingway's *The Sun Also Rises*

Political Issues in J.K. Rowling's Harry Potter Series

Racism in *The Autobiography of Malcolm X*

Racism in Harper Lee's *To Kill a Mockingbird*

Racism in Maya Angelou's *I Know Why the Caged Bird Sings*

Suicide in Arthur Miller's *Death of a Salesman*

Women's Issues in Amy Tan's *The Joy Luck Club*

Social Issues in Literature

Women's Issues in Nathaniel Hawthorne's *The Scarlet Letter*

Claudia Durst Johnson, Book Editor

GREENHAVEN PRESS
A part of Gale, Cengage Learning

Detroit • New York • San Francisco • New Haven, Conn • Waterville, Maine • London

Christine Nasso, *Publisher*
Elizabeth Des Chenes, *Managing Editor*

For more information, contact:
Greenhaven Press
27500 Drake Rd.
Farmington Hills, MI 48331-3535
Or you can visit our Internet site at gale.cengage.com

Articles in Greenhaven Press anthologies are often edited for length to meet page requirements. In addition, original titles of these works are changed to clearly present the main thesis and to explicitly indicate the author's opinion. Every effort is made to ensure that Greenhaven Press accurately reflects the original intent of the authors. Every effort has been made to trace the owners of copyrighted material.

Cover photograph reproduced by permission of Hulton Archive/Getty Images.

LIBRARY OF CONGRESS CATALOGING-IN-PUBLICATION DATA

Women's issues in Nathaniel Hawthorne's The scarlet letter / Claudia Durst Johnson, book editor.
p. cm. -- (Social issues in literature)
Includes bibliographical references and index.
ISBN-13: 978-0-7377-4262-6 (hbk.)
ISBN-13: 978-0-7377-4263-3 (pbk.)
1. Hawthorne, Nathaniel, 1804-1864. Scarlet letter. 2. Women in literature.
I. Johnson, Claudia D.
PS1868.W45 2008
813'.3--dc22

2008021502

Printed in the United States of America
1 2 3 4 5 6 7 13 12 11 10 09

Contents

Chapter 3: Contemporary Perspectives on Women's Issues

Introduction

Nathaniel Hawthorne's criticism of women writers and his social conservatism are puzzling when considered against his seemingly sympathetic portrait of Hester Prynne in his novel *The Scarlet Letter*. The result has spawned a range of critical interpretations of women's issues in Hawthorne's novel. An obvious difficulty arises from his well-known views on women writers (whom he scorned as a "damned mob of scribbling women"), his dissatisfaction with his sister-in-law's progressive views, and his disapproval of the way his friend the feminist journalist Margaret Fuller was living her life. These matters are hard to square with what appear to be Hester's sensitively rendered, radical statements about the need for a change in women's character and relationships. See Chapter 13, "Another View of Hester":

> As a first step, the whole system of society is to be torn down and built up anew. Then, the very nature of the opposite sex, or its long hereditary habit which has become like nature, is to be essentially modified before woman can be allowed to assume what seems a fair and suitable position.

The narrator's words here are describing the work Hester takes up at the end of her life—comforting suffering women. They also seem to allude to the struggle of Hawthorne's female contemporaries:

> She assured them, too, of her firm belief, that, at some brighter period, when the world should have grown ripe for it, in Heaven's own time, a new truth would be revealed, in order to establish the whole relation between man and woman on a surer ground of mutual happiness.

The interpretations of Hester Prynne presented in this volume are widely divergent: some authors see her as Hawthorne's rendering of a heroic woman, some stress her status as an outsider, and at least one—Louise DeSalvo—argues that, in the battle between the passionate woman and the hard-hearted patriarchy, Hawthorne allows his Puritan ancestors to win.

Both the time in which *The Scarlet Letter* is set (the mid-seventeenth century) and the time in which it was written (the mid-nineteenth century) are vital to a study of women's issues raised in the novel. The setting for the novel is Puritan New England, where notorious events occurred involving the persecution and execution of headstrong women. In 1637 Anne Hutchinson, about whom Hawthorne wrote an essay and who is mentioned in *The Scarlet Letter*, was found guilty of treason and heresy. Her crime was holding "mixed" meetings of men and women where she clarified and commented upon sermons. In 1660 Mary Dyer, member of the hated Quaker sect—which gave women a voice in religious meetings—was hanged on Boston Common when she persisted in returning to Boston to proselytize. The persecution of so-called witches in Massachusetts Bay chiefly targeted women.

These cases, along with a law passed in 1641 (by one of Hawthorne's ancestors) that made adultery punishable by death, form the background of *The Scarlet Letter*. Hester Prynne's adultery is committed just before the passage of the law. Her escape from the gallows is also explained by the fact that many Puritan magistrates disagreed with the harshness of the penalty and usually found ways to avoid upholding the death sentence. Still, Hester's punishment is much more lenient than the one that real female adulterers received.

By the nineteenth century, adulteresses were no longer executed or publicly whipped, but women were more repressed and limited in their sexuality. Puritans had a much more indulgent view of sex within marriage than did their nineteenth-century counterparts. Sex within marriage was viewed as a natural and expected pleasure for both men and women. Moreover, women in the Puritan community often joined their husbands in their professions and businesses and took over when their spouses became incapacitated or died.

At the time Hawthorne composed *The Scarlet Letter*, the prevailing belief was that decent women did not enjoy sex but submitted to it out of duty. Women were thus divided into two categories—Angels or Whores—and there was nothing in between. The complex character of Hester, however, fits into neither category; her letter *A* stands not only for "adulteress," but also for "angel," "able," and "artist."

In Hawthorne's own time, attitudes toward the nature of woman led to restrictions and inequities that needed redressing. Woman was viewed as a natural temptress. Her body and nature had to be hidden and constantly suppressed. It was generally held that a woman's use of her intellect drove her insane. It was useless and dangerous to educate her, so the education available to her was minimal. She was unfit for roles of leadership and management and was properly restricted to the home and the church. The professions, except for teaching, were closed to her. Like Hester, the genteel nineteenth-century woman had only needlework as a means of self-expression. And for the poor woman, it was often the means of survival.

It was in the decade before the publication of *The Scarlet Letter* that reformers, including Hawthorne's friends and relatives, began drawing attention to the limitations and injustices under which women suffered. The Grimké sisters (Sarah and Angelina), Lucy Stone, Susan B. Anthony, Amelia Bloomer, and Elizabeth Cady Stanton spoke at meetings (such an action was taboo in itself, no matter the message) in support of changes in women's position. In 1848, at a groundbreaking meeting in Seneca Falls, New York, women and their male supporters insisted on property rights for women whose inherited land automatically and legally was assumed by their husbands. Before the meeting was over, the issue of woman suffrage had been added.

The matters discussed in the following volume include the widely perceived nature of woman, society's idea of her proper place, the danger of her reformism and intellect, the impropriety of her assuming a role of leadership, her relationship to the church, and the matters of forced marriage and single motherhood.

Despite the impressive advances made by women since the nineteenth century, many issues raised in *The Scarlet Letter* are pertinent today.

Chronology

Nathaniel Hawthorne's Life

4 July 1804

Nathaniel Hawthorne is born.

1808

Hawthorne's father, a seaman, dies in Surinam, and his mother takes him to live with her family. His childhood is spent in Salem and Raymond, Maine.

1821–1825

Hawthorne attends Bowdoin College.

1825–1837

Hawthorne lives in Salem with his mother and sisters while trying to forge a career as a writer.

1828

Hawthorne anonymously publishes *Fanshawe*, a novel.

1830

Hawthorne publishes a sketch of Anne Hutchinson.

1832

Hawthorne publishes "The Gentle Boy," a story based on the Puritans' persecution of the Quakers.

1835

Hawthorne publishes "Young Goodman Brown," a short story dealing with the Puritans and witchcraft.

1837

"Twice-Told Tales," a collection of Hawthorne's previously published work, appears. Social reformer Elizabeth Peabody becomes his friend and introduces him to her sister, Sophia, to whom he becomes engaged in 1839.

1838

Hawthorne's story "Endicott and the Red Cross" mentions a young woman wearing a red letter *A* on her chest as punishment for adultery.

1839–1840

Hawthorne works at the Boston Custom House.

1841

For seven months Hawthorne lives in the Transcendentalist experimental community of Brook Farm.

1842

Hawthorne and Sophia Peabody are married. They move to Concord, Massachusetts, where they find feminist Margaret Fuller to be a congenial friend.

1845

Unable to make a living with his writing, Hawthorne returns to live in Salem with his mother and sisters, while Sophia lives with her parents in Boston.

1846

Another collection of short stories, *Mosses from an Old Manse*, is published, and Hawthorne secures a political position as a Custom House officer in Salem.

1849

Hawthorne is dismissed from the Custom House and begins work on *The Scarlet Letter*.

1850

The Hawthornes move to Lenox, Massachusetts, and *The Scarlet Letter* is published.

1851

The House of the Seven Gables and *The Snow Image, and Other Twice-Told Tales* are published.

1852

The Hawthornes buy a new home in Concord, Massachusetts. Hawthorne sees into print *The Blithedale Romance.*

1853–1857

The Hawthornes live in England, Nathaniel Hawthorne having received a political appointment as a consulate to Liverpool from U.S. President Franklin Pierce, his college friend.

1857–1859

Hawthorne loses his job when Franklin Pierce leaves office; the family spends this time in Italy.

1859

The Hawthornes return to England.

1860

The Marble Faun is published. The Hawthornes leave England and move back to Concord, Massachusetts.

19 May 1864

Hawthorne dies.

Social Issues in Literature

Chapter 1

Background on Nathaniel Hawthorne

The Life of Nathaniel Hawthorne

John L. Idol Jr.

John L. Idol Jr. is a distinguished alumni professor emeritus of English at Clemson University, a founding member of the Nathaniel Hawthorne Society, former editor of the Nathaniel Hawthorne Review, *and the author of books and articles on Hawthorne.*

Hawthorne's father died when Nathaniel was three, leaving him surrounded by women throughout his childhood and adolescence. His boyhood world consisted of his mother and two sisters. He was only separated from that woman's world twice: first to be schooled in Salem while his family lived in Maine, and later to attend Bowdoin College in Maine (during which time his family moved back to Salem). Although he loved Maine, he felt deserted by his mother. After graduating from college, he returned to live in Salem with his mother and sisters for about ten years. Three of his good friends were independent-minded women: his wife's sister, Elizabeth Peabody, who was actively involved in reform movements; Margaret Fuller, author of Nineteenth-Century Women; *and Francis Kemble, a former actress and a formidable woman. Even before his marriage to Sophia Peabody, Hawthorne received help from Elizabeth Peabody in securing publication for some of his work. Sophia, Nathaniel's wife, was a physically frail but intellectually strong woman and his supporter and closest friend.*

Although Nathaniel Hawthorne called himself "the obscurest man in American letters," his achievements in fiction, both as short-story writer and novelist, offer models fashioned

John L. Idol Jr. *Dictionary of Literary Biography*. Belmont, CA: The Gale Group, 2000.

too well for contemporary and later writers to ignore. Even though fame was slow to come and his wallet remained relatively thin throughout his career as a writer, Hawthorne claimed a central place in American letters, becoming, in time, an influential force in the artistic development of such writers as Herman Melville, Henry James, William Dean Howells, Mary Jane Wilkins Freeman, Sarah Orne Jewett, William Faulkner, and Flannery O'Connor, members of the so-called Hawthorne School. His focus on the past of the nation, especially the Puritan era, his delving into the social and psychological forces underlying human behavior, his reliance on symbols to convey rich and ambivalent value to his stories and romances, his insistence on finding and understanding the sources of humanity's darker side, and his exploration of such themes as isolation, monomania, guilt, concealment, social reform, and redemption not only created a following among aspiring writers but also brought him into the nation's classrooms, where *The Scarlet Letter* (1850), to name only his most famous work, still holds a firm place: more than eighty editions of it are available in formats ranging from textbooks, casebooks, and paperbacks to audio cassettes and CD-ROMs.

A Household of Women

Born 4 July 1804 in Salem, Massachusetts, Nathaniel Hawthorne (who added a "W" to the family name) was the middle child of Nathaniel and Elizabeth Manning Hathorne, who also had two daughters, Elizabeth and Louisa. Young Nathaniel was a descendant of Puritan settlers in Salem and the adjoining communities. His father, captain of a ship, died in 1808 in Surinam (Dutch Guiana) of yellow fever. Lacking funds to maintain her own household, Elizabeth Manning Hathorne retreated to her parents' home and looked to her Manning relatives for support. Reclusive by nature, she remained a widow, living in Salem except for the years she removed her family to Raymond, Maine, where her brother built her a house and where Nathaniel "ran quite wild" as he skated, fished, and hunted. Before making that move, she had begun Nathaniel's education at home, placing him (because of a leg injury he suffered while playing ball) under the tutelage of Joseph Emerson Worcester. That injury helped to fashion his personality, since he became a reader, continuing to read assiduously, especially on rainy days in Raymond, such authors as John Bunyan and William Shakespeare and acquired, as he later lamented, his "cursed habits of solitude." To prepare him for college, his mother sent him back to Salem, where, living with his Manning relatives, he studied with Benjamin Lynde Oliver, a lawyer. As a means of entertaining himself, his absent mother, and his Manning kin, he launched a newspaper, *The Spectator*, imitating the famous journal of Richard Steele and Joseph Addison and serving as writer, editor, printer (done by careful hand-lettering), and publisher. In it he shared short essays, included some family gossip, made his debut as a poet, and created a comic classified notice aimed at finding a husband for his Aunt Mary. This short-lived project had to be produced in his spare time, since he served as both secretary and bookkeeper in Uncle William Manning's stagecoach office and pressed forward with his preparatory studies. This experience in the workaday world revealed something important to him, as he told his sister Ebe: "No man can be a Poet and a Book Keeper at the same time." (When he became a writer, he produced little creative work while holding down jobs in a customhouse or in a consular office.)

So that he could be closer to his mother and sisters, Hawthorne chose the frontier college of Bowdoin, enrolling there in 1821. . . .

Preceding his graduation, his mother and sisters had returned to Salem, where he now joined them in 1825, spending the decade that followed in a "dismal and squalid chamber" in his pursuit of literary fame. . . .

Female Assistance

Hawthorne spent roughly a decade (1825–1835) writing, submitting, receiving rejection notices, and, in moments of frustration, burning manuscripts. Excepting evening strolls, occasional hiking tours, and walks along the seashore, he saw little of the world. A temporary break in his routine came in January 1836, when he accepted appointment as editor of *The American Magazine of Useful and Entertaining Knowledge*, located in Boston. He and his sister Elizabeth wrote most of the copy. By June the publisher was bankrupt, and Hawthorne returned to Salem. Writing to Longfellow to account for the time since their last meeting, Hawthorne confided: "I have secluded myself from society; and yet I never meant any such thing, nor dreamed of the sort of life I was going to lead. I have made a captive of myself and put me in a dungeon; and now I cannot find the key to let myself out." Yet, he wanted the tales to reach beyond his dungeon, "to open an intercourse with the world," as he suggested in his preface to the 1851 republication of *Twice-told Tales*. But intercourse came on its own terms, more through his tales and sketches than through confessional autobiographical prefaces, a point he later insisted upon in his conclusion to the preface for *Mosses from an Old Manse*: "So far as I am a man of really individual attributes, I veil my face; nor am I, nor have ever been one of those supremely hospitable people, who serve up their hearts delicately fried, with brain-sauce, as a tidbit for their beloved public."

If he had paused to consider how the publication of *Twice-Told Tales* affected one of his Salem neighbors, he could have credited the book with helping fashion the key that unlocked his dungeon door. Once disabused of her assumption that one of Hawthorne's sisters was the author of the book, neighbor Elizabeth Palmer Peabody became the champion of the volume, reviewing it for *The New-Yorker* (24 March 1838) and recommending it to her Boston and Concord friends, includ-

The House of Seven Gables, now an historic site in Salem, Massachusetts, was an inspiration for Nathaniel Hawthorne's novel, The House of Seven Gables. *The dresser pictured housed the manuscripts of* The Scarlet Letter. AP Images.

ing Ralph Waldo Emerson. Her efforts to draw the Hawthorne siblings within her social and intellectual circle ultimately brought her semi-invalid sister, Sophia Amelia Peabody, and Hawthorne together. Intent upon furthering his career and hoping to enlist him to write children's literature, Elizabeth Palmer Peabody encouraged Hawthorne's interest in writing historical accounts of New England's past for children. . . .

He . . . asked Sophia to do a courageous thing: to marry him, combine their talents (hers was in copying as well as producing paintings), and move to Concord to the Old Manse, the home of Emerson's grandfather and step-grandfather. They took their wedding vows 9 July 1842 and, once settled into the house, considered themselves a new Adam and Eve in Eden. Here was a garden ready planted for them, thanks to Henry David Thoreau, and here were such companions as Emerson, Ellery Channing, Bronson Alcott, and Margaret Fuller to engage in conversations or go hiking or boating with. The Old Manse was their home for three and a half years. Hawthorne entered one of his most productive periods, writing twenty sketches and tales, and celebrated with Sophia the birth of a daughter, Una on 3 March 1844. . . .

Excellent though they were, these and other pieces written during the Old Manse period failed to earn sufficient income for the Hawthornes to pay their bills. After trying to obtain a political appointment for a position in Salem's post office, Hawthorne turned to his political friends once again, this time winning appointment as surveyor in the Salem Custom House. His family shared living quarters with his mother and sister before he was able to rent a house and provide a separate apartment for them. Work at the Custom House occupied his mornings, but he did find time to assemble twenty-one uncollected stories and present them as *Mosses from an Old Manse* together with one of his most significant familiar essays, "The Old Manse," which provides an idyllic glance at his Edenic life in the famous old parsonage.

Life in Salem proved anything but pleasant. A dying seaport, Salem hosted a customhouse filled with appointees with little or nothing to do. They idled their time away, as Hawthorne humorously revealed in an essay on the customhouse published as an introduction to *The Scarlet Letter*. But boredom is a minor thing compared to the loss of a job. The election of Zachary Taylor meant that the Whigs could replace Democratic appointees if they so chose. Acting against arguments by Hawthorne's literary and political friends that the nation's intellectual and cultural life would be better served if he were to retain his post, Hawthorne's political foes, led by Charles Wentworth Upham, dismissed him.

The Mother

Downcast as he was over the loss of his position and his income, Hawthorne had a heavier blow to endure, the death of his mother on 31 July 1849, "the darkest hour I ever lived." His notebook entries record the depth of his pain and suffering even as he describes the heedless playfulness of Una and Julian (born after the move to Salem) as they reenact their grandmother's dying gestures.

The intensity and force of the prose in his notebook was a prelude to the work that Hawthorne began soon thereafter, *The Scarlet Letter*. Living on funds that Sophia had stashed away, Hawthorne returned to the Puritan past that had so absorbed him in the earliest stages of his writing career in such tales as "Endicott and the Red Cross," where he noted the penalty invoked for adultery (the wearing of the letter "A"), "The Gray Champion," "The May-Pole of Merry Mount," "The Gentle Boy," and "Young Goodman Brown."

Choosing adultery as the sin to which the Puritans were to react, and in so doing, according to some of his moralistic critics, "Frenchifying" American literature, Hawthorne presented the story of a young wife, Hester, who, separated from her much older husband, Chillingworth, falls in love with her minister, Dimmesdale, and bears a child, whom she names Pearl. Intent upon punishing Hester and discovering her partner in sin, the Puritans force her to wear a scarlet "A" on her bosom and demand that she reveal her lover's name. In their treatment of her, the church leaders of Salem, where the action is set, and their followers mete out punishment with mean-spirited, intolerant rigor but are flexible enough, eventually, to see worth in her as seamstress, nurse, and conscientious mother. . . .

Hawthorne thus sets in motion forces that play themselves out with staggering impact, the earliest example of its power coming when Hawthorne read the just completed romance to his wife. He recorded that hearing him read it, with his voice swelling and heaving as if he "were tossed up and down on an ocean," provoked such strong feelings that "it broke her heart and sent her to bed with a grievous headache." At least she realized, though, that she had just heard a powerful piece of literature; as Henry James was to declare a generation later: "The book was the finest piece of imaginative writing yet put forth in this country."

Hawthorne's Family's Impact on His Fiction

Gloria C. Erlich

Gloria C. Erlich founded the Princeton Research Forum and the National Coalition of Independent Scholars. Her writings include the books Family Themes and Hawthorne's Fiction *(1984) and* The Sexual Education of Edith Wharton *(1992).*

The issues of single motherhood, woman's intellectual independence, and female eroticism in Hawthorne's fiction are, in Gloria C. Erlich's psychological analysis, seen as issuing from his relationship to his mother, his two sisters, and his wife. His weak mother, to whom he had strong emotional ties, was the opposite of the strong Hester Prynne. She yielded to the authority of her brother Robert, who wanted to send the boy to school in Salem while she and her daughters remained in Maine. In contrast, Hester defiantly challenges the local male authorities when they attempt to take Pearl away from her. Hawthorne's sister Elizabeth provided him with the material for Hester's independent-mindedness, raising the issues of heterodoxy and intellectual independence in woman, at a time when women were supposed to accept, without question, the ideas of their male leaders. Finally, Hawthorne's wife, Sophia, contributed to the idea of woman, represented by Hester, as a full and complex human being who is both sexual and angelic, contrary to the prevailing views of women at the time.

From the pressure of Manning [Hawthorne's mother's family] values and personalities, Nathaniel sought refuge in the inner circle of his own family. The Hawthorne women accepted him as he was and even adored him for the very traits

Gloria C. Erlich, *Family Themes and Hawthorne's Fiction: The Tenacious Web*. Piscataway, NJ: Rutgers University Press, 1984.

others wished to alter. His mother and sisters [Louisa and Elizabeth, whose nickname was Ebe] catered to his moods, whether for poetry, indolence, or "gunning" in the wilds of Raymond [Maine]. Their uncritical acceptance was sorely missed during the years of separation. He longed for and idealized his mother's and Louisa's compliance and Ebe's intellectual stimulation. How different from the Mannings' prodding criticism was Ebe's judgment that Nathaniel would "never *do* anything; he is an ideal person" and Louisa's "my brother is never idle." Only in marriage to the adoring Sophia was he later able to reexperience and secure to himself such uncritical acceptance.

Although united in admiration of Nathaniel, Madame Hawthorne, Ebe, and Louisa had markedly distinct personalities. Each played a different role in his psychic economy and each contributed to his attitudes toward women. In exploring these roles and contributions we move from the mother, inmost center of the family circle, outward to the two contrasting sisters. En route we observe how metamorphoses of these primary female images link up with received literary traditions and emerge revitalized in Hawthorne's fiction. . . .

Longing for Mother

Elizabeth Hawthorne did not deny herself to her son, but she allowed Uncle Robert [Robert Manning, her brother] to take him away from her and from the beloved Raymond home. The boy came to feel that he was being managed, played upon, and manipulated by the uncle who seemed so often to step between himself and his mother. In the Herbert Street days [when Elizabeth and her children lived at her parents' house in Salem], Uncle Robert took Nathaniel out of the room he shared with his mother and sisters and into Robert's own bed. During the Raymond period the sisters were allowed for the most part to remain with their mother, whereas Nathaniel was sent back to Salem. Little wonder that he sometimes wished that he might have been a girl and pinned to his mother's apron. In Raymond was all that he loved—his mother, Sebago Lake, and the wild free life. What Ebe called "the fatality" that brought the family back to Salem despite all their resolutions and intentions was, in Nathaniel's case, Uncle Robert.

Nathaniel's emotional life was genuinely split between what he wanted for himself and what the Mannings wanted for him, between what he felt to be the legitimate authority of his mother and the inexplicably effective authority of Uncle Robert, between Salem, where fate, practical necessity, and Manning authority placed him, and Raymond, where he longed to be. . . .

In a letter of complaint about scolding and unpleasantness in the Manning household, fifteen-year-old Nathaniel mourns the lost symbiosis of his childhood: "Oh how I wish I was again with you, with nothing to do but go agunning. But the happiest days of my life are gone. Why was I not a girl that I might have been pinned all my life to my mother's apron."

A year older and ready to depart for college, he seems to have regressed even further and become more openly competitive with his uncle. He wrote to his mother:

> I shall probably see you in September, and stay 4 weeks with you. I hope you will remain in Raymond during the time I am at college, and then I can be with you 3 months out of the year. . . . It is now going on two Years since I saw you. Do not you regret the time when I was a little boy. I do almost. I [am] now as tall as Uncle Robert. . . . Do not show this to Uncle Richard.
>
> Your Affectionate Son,
>
> Nathaniel Hathorne

Such nostalgia for childhood dependency persisting into late adolescence indicates serious problems with gender identity and too close a relationship with the mother. They show why Uncle Robert felt it to be precisely his duty to untie the lad from the maternal apron. This salutary task was to prove a thankless one. It rekindled hostility toward the intervening uncle and intensified longing for and idealization of the distant mother. At an age when other interests and objects would normally have been replacing primary ones, when the youth might have been straining forward and outward from the family for love and confirmation of identity, Nathaniel sought security in the past. This regression delayed many kinds of maturation, including development of a confident masculinity. Not too surprising, then, is his later choice of little Pearl, who was always at her mother's side, to represent his never wholly satisfied longing for symbiosis with the mother.

Mother and son missed each other intensely. The mother seemed to accept the separation fatalistically, whereas Nathaniel expressed his sense of deprivation frequently throughout the period of enforced separation. It contributed to his dislike of school, his resentment of the authority of his aunts and Uncle Robert, and most especially to his passionate desire to be "lord of himself," which he reiterated throughout the period of enforced separation.

The Strong Single Mother

An important fictional representation of the dissociation between home and parents appears in [Hawthorne's story] "The Gentle Boy," written around 1829, fairly early in the "long seclusion" in his mother's home after returning from college. At its center is Ilbrahim, a small boy passing from the care of his natural parents into that of a surrogate family. The situation is of special significance because it accounts for the loss of original parents and features the relationship between a boy and his mother.

Historically grounded in the conflict between Puritans and Quakers in the seventeenth century, the story presents mother-son figurations rather than realistic portraits. The gentle boy

Nathaniel Hawthorne, the descendent of strict and influential Puritans, explored women's issues in The Scarlet Letter. Public Domain.

of this violent story is the artist as a wounded child, and his Quaker mother Catharine is a mother-figure as different from Hawthorne's own mother as is Hester Prynne. In both strong-willed fictional mothers Hawthorne created counterimages, negatives, of his own mother, endowing them with passion, self-direction, and personal magnetism. Bearing marked similarities as powerful females and single mothers, Hester and

Catharine nevertheless differ significantly in the quality of their mothering, for Hester is mother to a daughter and Catharine to a son. Hester keeps her daughter near her and subordinates expression of her individual selfhood to maternal duty. Pearl and Hester are inseparable. In contrast, Catharine clearly values expression of her own ideas more highly than she values the maternal bond. Acting out her own needs, she permits separation from her son. . . .

Feminity and Free Thinking

Antithetical female types, staples of Gothic romance, were filled out by Hawthorne's experience of his own two sisters. They were markedly different in personality and experience. Maria Louisa, the younger sister, has often been described as fun-loving, amiable, and ordinary. She liked dancing, parties, and pretty clothes. A capable cook and an excellent seamstress, she yet would accompany Nathaniel in his hunting and fishing in Raymond. She helped him compose his neo-Augustan [newspaper] *Spectator* and belonged to his secret Pin Society. Sociable and affectionate, she loved plants and animals, was very "feminine" in the nineteenth-century sense and yet always girlish in her sense of herself. With all her domesticity, she apparently never considered marrying.

In contrast to her brilliant older sister and brother, she has seemed ordinary to biographers looking for drama. Nevertheless, her homely virtues influenced Hawthorne's conception of the domestic Phoebe type, the fair woman whom the artist may marry in order to bring himself back within the bounds of society. Unlike her older sister, Maria Louisa was accepting almost to the point of passivity, and companionable without presenting intellectual challenge or competition. Her letters were mostly about her flowers and pets, dancing, and parties.

Elizabeth Manning Hawthorne, or Ebe, on the other hand was dark-haired, beautiful, imperious, opinionated, and brilliant. In [Sophia's sister] Elizabeth Peabody's recollections, she seemed a "brilliant little girl" who became "a great genius . . . her bright rather shy eyes, and a rather excited frequent low laugh, looked full of wit and keenness—as if she were experienced in the world; not the least sentimental in air, but strongly intellectual." She was a precocious child, and even her earliest letters show mastery of English prose. These early letters are tart, rather pert, critical of people, and impatient with even the conventions of letter writing. . . .

From his sister Ebe, Hawthorne's imagination drew traits for his dark women—imperious pride, beauty, and intellectual gifts. . . .

For Hawthorne, the mother's seductive image merged with Ebe's incestuous aura, the two Elizabeths thus combining to create a maternal figure of dangerous sensuality. The mother was the catalytic element that made possible the fusion of all the early female images into Hester Prynne, Hawthorne's most complex literary character. . . .

Sexuality and Innocence

In Sophia, Hawthorne found qualities both necessary and familiar. He had grown accustomed to and required female adoration as support for his fragile self-esteem, and his sisters, who never looked to other men, had supplied this for far too long. Sophia was fully prepared to take over this function. Moreover, her virginal, sisterly-daughterly demeanor was peculiarly compatible with his earliest impression of womanhood.

The brevity of his mother's marriage and her rapid reversion to the role of sister and daughter on her return to the parental home made her seem to him a celibate, asexual figure. This essentially virginal image, paradoxically like the "image of Divine Maternity" evoked by Hester on the scaffold, led him to locate the erotic in the "sacred image of sinless motherhood." The icon of the Virgin Mother, fusing innocence with mysterious sexuality, was the inner standard that made Sophia's maidenly reserve almost immediately familiar and desirable to him.

Having qualities continuous with his earliest needs and fantasies, Sophia served as his ideal anima figure [in Jungian psychology, anima is the feminine part of a male personality], helping to direct these into more adult channels of sexuality and creativity. To a remarkable degree she fits Daniel Levinson's version of the anima figure as "special woman": "She shares [the Dream], believes in him as its hero, gives it her blessing, joins him on the journey and creates a 'boundary space' within which his aspirations can be imagined and his hopes nourished.... [She] can foster his adult aspirations while accepting his dependency, his incompleteness and his need to make her into something more than (and less than) she actually is." Victorian stereotypes of the angelic woman also helped Sophia fulfill a role for which she was peculiarly fitted by experience and temperament....

Sophia filled Nathaniel's particularly intense needs for home, an anchor, and validation as lover and artist. Like his first women, she granted priority to his wishes and whims and affirmed the importance of his work. Beyond that, she gave him what mother and sisters could not, of course, provide, which was appropriate confirmation of his manhood as a lover and a father of children.

All this Sophia performed remarkably well, especially in view of her own and her husband's unusual histories before marriage. For one who had been so long a petted invalid, she adapted with impressive speed to the roles of wife and mother. Her need for an idol and his need for adoration complemented each other beautifully, stimulating her ability to create a "home-feeling" that spoke to his deepest unfulfilled longings....

The successful union of such unusual people as Sophia and Nathaniel Hawthorne indicates that an adequate foundation for intimacy must have been prepared. No matter that his mother appears to have given up on her own life and to have abdicated much of her parental role. She must have been at very least a good enough mother to have generated in her son the adaptive capacity to emerge from depression and isolation, to love and satisfy a woman, to make lifelong friends, and to cope with the difficult terms of life as an artist-provider.

The Hawthorne-Fuller Friendship

David B. Kesterson

David B. Kesterson, professor of English at the University of North Texas, is a cofounder of the Nathaniel Hawthorne Society, its first president, and editor of Critical Essays on Hawthorne's "The Scarlet Letter" *(1988).*

Margaret Fuller, author of one of America's first feminist texts, has often been considered as one of the models for Hester Prynne. Her character also contributes to Hawthorne's protagonists in other novels. Fuller and Hawthorne met nine or ten years before the publication of The Scarlet Letter. *They continued to be close friends until a few years before her death in a shipwreck in 1850. Like Hester, Fuller reportedly conceived a child out of wedlock, though she was married to her son's father at the time of her death. Hawthorne came to know Fuller well when both lived at the Transcendental utopian community of Brook Farm and continued a closer friendship when the Hawthornes moved to Concord, Massachusetts. In her notebooks, letters, and published reviews, she spoke highly of his character and his fiction, and in 1845 Hawthorne and Sophia wrote Fuller a congratulatory letter on her publication of* Women in the Nineteenth Century. *But Hawthorne's admiration of Fuller came to be mixed with animosity, especially after she moved to Italy.*

We do not know exactly when Sarah Margaret Fuller and Nathaniel Hawthorne met, but it was probably in 1840 or early 1841, before their encounter at Brook Farm in the spring and summer of 1841. Much has been written about the relationship of Fuller and Hawthorne, a puzzling friendship

David B. Kesterson, *Hawthorne and Women*. Amherst: University of Massachusetts Press, 1999.

that emits mixed signals. From the written record it is evident that the warm feelings of friendship often expressed by both individuals were more ardent on Fuller's side than Hawthorne's.

A Close Relationship

Many passages in Fuller's journals and letters speak to her great admiration of Hawthorne and feeling of friendship with him and his wife Sophia as well. As early in their relationship as June 1842, when she had learned from Sophia Peabody of her impending marriage to Hawthorne, Fuller responded to Sophia that she would find herself very happy, "for if ever I saw a man who combined delicate tenderness to understand the heart of a woman, with quiet depth and manliness enough to satisfy her, it is Mr. Hawthorne." In the same month, writing to [Transcendentalist thinker Ralph Waldo] Emerson about the Hawthornes' imminent move to Concord, she assured the Concord sage that "I think you must take pleasure in Hawthorne when yo[u] know him, you will find him more mellow than most fruits at your board, and of distinct flavor too." And we know that Fuller visited the Hawthornes extensively during their first two years in Concord at the Old Manse (from 1842 until late 1844), always commenting on the pleasantness of those visits and the exhilaration she found in them. On 19 August 1842, she confided to her journal:

> Went to see the Hawthornes: it was very pleasant. The poplars whisper so suddenly in the avenue their pleasant tale, and every where the view is so peaceful. The house within I like, all their things are so expressive of themselves and mix in so gracefully with the old furniture. H. walked home with me: we stopped some time to look at the moon[;] she was struggling with clouds. H said he should be much more willing to die than two months ago, for he had had some real possession in life, but still he never wished to leave this

> earth: it was beautiful enough. He expressed, as he always does, many fine perceptions. I like to hear the lightest thing he says[.]

From several passages such as this, it appears that Fuller's feelings toward Hawthorne were warm, enthusiastic, and open. No reserve is indicated.

Hawthorne's part in the friendship was reciprocal to a degree, but certainly he was not so wholly forthcoming as Fuller. We know that he devoted some time to the friendship while he lived at the Old Manse, walking with Fuller in the nearby woods, taking her canoeing on the Concord River, and inviting her to visit him and Sophia whenever she was in town. He apparently felt he could confide in her. Responding by letter to her bold request that he and Sophia, only one month wed, take in Fuller's sister Ellen and brother-in-law Ellery Channing as boarders at the Manse, Hawthorne politely demurred, gave his reasons, then assured her, "There is nobody to whom I would more willingly speak my mind, because I can be certain of being thoroughly understood." And when, a year later, Fuller tried again to get the Hawthornes to open their home—this time to friend Charles Newcomb—Hawthorne again refused, but wrote that he found it easier to give her a "negative" than to other people "because you do not peep at matters through a narrow chink, but can take my view as perfectly as your own." In the same letter he confides in Fuller about his personal activity that winter, sharing with her his joys of ice skating and of his and Sophia's close companionship.

There are, however, those other puzzling remarks Hawthorne made about Fuller that are equivocal, uncomplimentary, or occasionally outright condemnatory. He commented about her garrulousness, for example. . . .

Although the Hawthorne/Fuller personal relationship is an interesting, if somewhat disquieting one and deserves more attention, my purpose here is to focus on their literary relationship, specifically on Fuller's critical reaction to Hawthorne's works. Her commentary is limited to only four of Hawthorne's collections of tales and sketches prior to 1850. Fuller, we recall, died in 1850, only a few months after Hawthorne's first major novel, *The Scarlet Letter*, was published. . . .

Fuller's Reviews of Hawthorne's Early Work

[Writing in the July 1842 issue of *Dial*,] Fuller singles out with pleasure three new sketches in [the] second edition of *Twice-told Tales*, "The Village Uncle," "The Lily's Quest," and "Chippings with a Chisel," and again admires the "sweet grace" of "Footprints on the Seashore." The most successful tales, she feels, are the more realistic sketches, ones that she terms the "studies of familiar life." . . .

There was a lapse of four years before Fuller wrote again about Hawthorne. Much had changed in her life by then. She had been lured away from Boston to New York in late 1844 by Horace Greeley, editor of the *New-York Daily Tribune*, to write review articles for his newspaper. It appeared that Fuller had found the slot for which she was best suited, up to this point in her life, because her literary accomplishment during the nearly two years she was in New York was remarkable. She published two books—*Woman in the Nineteenth Century* (Feb. 1845) and *Papers on Literature and Art* (Aug. 1846)—and some 250 essays for the *Tribune*. . . .

Fuller's only review of Hawthorne in the *Tribune* was of *Mosses from an Old Manse*, prominently displayed in its entirety on the front page of the 22 June 1846 issue. . . .

"Young Goodman Brown" . . . is the tale from *Mosses* that draws most of Fuller's commentary in the *Tribune* review. It is a story that discloses the "secret of the breast." Reading it as depicting a universal experience, Fuller wonders who has not had the dismaying jolt so forcefully portrayed in the story: the "hour of anguish, when the old familiar faces grow dark and dim in the lurid light—when the gods of the hearth, honored in childhood, adored in youth, crumble, and nothing, nothing is left which the daily earthly feelings can embrace—can cherish with unbroken Faith!" Some people, however, survive this shock of recognition "more happily" than Goodman Brown; those who "have not sought it—have never of their own accord walked forth with the Temptor into the dim shades of Doubt." . . .

As mentioned above, Margaret Fuller did not live to read and review Hawthorne's major works of the 1850s: *The Scarlet Letter, The House of the Seven Gables, The Blithedale Romance* . . . , and *The Marble Faun* in 1860. The ship bearing her, her husband Count Giovanni Ossoli, and their young son wrecked and sank on 19 July 1850 off Fire Island, New York, as Fuller was returning to America from Italy, where she had lived for three years. All three of the Ossolis were drowned. . . .

A Response to Fuller's Feminist Book

Hawthorne's personal relationship with Margaret Fuller remains a puzzle never to be completely solved. But as literary friends and acquaintances the record is clear that there was mutual respect and admiration between them (Hawthorne and Sophia even wrote Fuller a letter of congratulations in 1845 on the publication of *Woman in the Nineteenth Century*). As for her literary criticism of Hawthorne, Margaret Fuller's keen mind fastened on those traits that are so legendarily Hawthornesque—from his "soft grace" and ease of style to his "genial human sense," to his quietude and repose, to a "great reserve of thought and strength," to the deep, probing portraits that conceal as much as they reveal.

Chapter 2

The Scarlet Letter and Women's Issues

Hester and Feminists of the 1840s

David S. Reynolds

David S. Reynolds is Distinguished Professor of English and American Studies at Baruch College and the Graduate Center of the City University of New York. Among his books are Beneath the American Renaissance *(1988),* Walt Whitman's America *(1995), and* Serpent in the Cup *(1997).*

During the 1840s, when Hawthorne created the character of Hester Prynne, feminists were challenging societal attitudes toward women. The first women's rights convention, for instance, was held in 1848 at Seneca Falls, New York, and marked the start of the woman suffrage movement. According to Reynolds, the difference between Hester and other female portraits of the time is her complex combination of conflicting qualities and her reflection of the gender politics of the suffragettes. She is both a dark, fallen woman and a moral heroine who finds true redemption and devotes her life to the needy, especially women. She turns the meaning of her letter A *from "adulteress" to "able," challenging the nineteenth-century division of women into either devils or angels. Hawthorne uses Hester to address not only the frequent unhappiness of domestic life but also the limitations on women: as was true of many women in the 1840s, the only way Hester can make a living is as a seamstress.*

Although Hawthorne is generally credited with having created the most intriguing heroines in pre-Civil War litera-

David S. Reynolds, *Beneath the American Renaissance: The Subversive Imagination in the Age of Emerson and Melville*. New York: Alfred A. Knopf, 1988.

ture, little has been said about the relationship between these heroines and the women's culture of the day. The fact is that the rich variety of female character types in antebellum popular culture prepared the way for Hawthorne's complex heroines. Hawthorne's best fiction occupies an energetic middle space between the Conventional novel and the literature of women's wrongs. Skeptical of the Conventional and politically uncommitted, Hawthorne was in an ideal position to choose judiciously from the numerous female stereotypes and to assimilate them in literary texts. His career illustrates the success of an especially responsive author in gathering together disparate female types and recombining them artistically so that they became crucial elements of the rhetorical and artistic construct of his fiction.

As a creator of heroines, Hawthorne began as an unusually flexible but rather haphazard experimenter with various native and foreign character types. His earliest fiction, published between 1828 and 1837, can be distinguished from that of other American authors by the heterogeneity of its heroines. None of his early tales contains a heroine that can be called complex, but, taken as a whole, the tales are a remarkable testament to Hawthorne's ability to escape narrow, monolithic views of women. On the one hand, he proved himself capable of producing redemptive moral exemplars: in "Little Annie's Ramble" an angelic child revives and cheers an old man; "The Village Uncle" features a bright, sunshiny woman; in "The Vision of the Fountain" an angelic exemplar is the visionary creation of a narrator's fancy. On the other hand, he also gave graphic portrayals of female criminals, such as the wandering heroine who has cruelly abandoned her family in "The Hollow of Three Hills," and women victims, such as the persecuted Quaker woman in "The Gentle Boy" and the Puritan adulteress forced to wear a scarlet A in "Endicott and the Red Cross."

Gender-Specific Themes

His most complex early use of women characters occurs in "Young Goodman Brown," in which the affirmative values embodied in the allegorically named exemplar, Faith, are shattered by the protagonist's recognition of universal sinfulness, represented by the gathering of saints and sinners in the forest. In previous chapters we have seen that "Young Goodman Brown" was in many senses a representative 1830s piece whose ambiguities owed much to dark popular writings of the decade. It also drew on the ironic perception of the underlying similarity of respectable and fallen women that was being discussed in reform writings. When Hawthorne describes "chaste dames and dewy virgins" consorting with "women of spotted fame" and when he mentions outwardly good women who kill their babies or husbands, he is tapping ironies that surrounded fallen women and women criminals in several popular works of the 1830s. When he has the angelic Faith appear at this demonic gathering, he dramatically undercuts the power of the moral exemplar. For the first time in his fiction, real density of meaning surrounds his heroines because he boldly brings together under one fictional roof moral exemplars, fallen women, and women criminals, a combination that produces an explosion of ironic meaning. The explosion is all the more powerful because Hawthorne uses a Puritan setting, so that the contemporary ironies take on a universality and a resonance because they are treated with Calvinistic seriousness. It must be emphasized, however, that here Hawthorne creates a *combination* of character types but not a real *fusion*, as he would in more interesting later heroines. His portrayal of various kinds of women in a single tale is significant but is finally subordinated to his main purpose of studying the disillusionment of Young Goodman Brown himself.

In short, his early tales reveal his remarkable openness to various character types, his occasional success in bringing together different types in a single tale, but his minimization of gender-specific themes. It was only in the early 1840s that his fiction revealed his growing awareness of both women's wrongs and women's rights. It was during this period, we should recall, that he spent time at Brook Farm among progressive thinkers, including the period's leading feminist theorist, Margaret Fuller. His exposure to feminist ideas during a time of economic depression and widespread exploitation of working women had a strong impact upon his fiction. Unlike Catharine Sedgwick, he did not blithely dismiss the sufferings of American working women. He succinctly but powerfully registered the sufferings of seamstresses in "The Procession of Life" (1843), which contains the following alarmed description: "But what is this crowd of pale-cheeked, slender girls, who disturb the ear with the multiplicity of their short, dry coughs? They are seamstresses, who have plied the daily and nightly needle in the service of master-tailors and close-fisted contractors, until now it is almost time for each to hem the borders of her own shroud." In "The Christmas Banquet" (1844), a dark tale about an imagined gathering of the most wretched people on earth, Hawthorne shows that his sympathy extends not only to seamstresses but to all women victimized by overwhelming wrongs against their sex. Among the guests at the sad Christmas banquet are two women: "one, a half-starved, consumptive seamstress, the representative of thousands just as wretched; the other, a woman of unemployed energy, who found herself in the world with nothing to achieve, nothing to enjoy, and nothing even to suffer. She had, therefore, driven herself to the verge of madness by dark broodings over the wrongs of her sex, and its exclusion from a proper field of action."

While these tales reveal his new sensitivity to women's wrongs, other tales of the period demonstrate his simultaneous recognition of women's rights. Among the reformers who appear in "Earth's Holocaust" (1844) are a number of women who propose to fling into the bonfire their petticoats

In this scene from the movie The Scarlet Letter, *Hester Prynne (played by Lillian Gish) stands on a platform surrounded by townspeople, while Arthur Dimmesdale (played by Lars Hanson) reveals a scarlet "A" on his own chest. Hawthorne's* The Scarlet Letter *challenged society's attitudes toward women.* Springer/Corbis-Bettmann.

and gowns, "and assume the garb, together with the manners, duties, offices, and responsibilities of the opposite sex." Although here Hawthorne gently satirizes public agitation for women's rights, in "The New Adam and Eve" (1843) he endorses a kind of moral exemplar feminism when, imagining the wholesome Eve sitting in an American legislative hall, he writes: "Man's intellect, moderated by Woman's tenderness and moral sense! Were such the legislation of the world, there would be no need of State Houses, Capitols, Halls of Parliament." A new political consciousness, therefore, characterized his fictional treatment of women in the early 1840s.

Hester's Precursors

By 1844 Hawthorne was in a unique position among American authors dealing with women's issues. No other American writer had approached him in producing so large a variety of fictional heroines, from his heterogeneous characters of the 1830s to his more topical, socially representative heroines of the early 1840s. He was now ready to produce a heroine who fused opposite qualities and thus assumed stature as a truly complex, memorable literary character. All his earlier tales had achieved *combinations* of different types of heroines but not *fusions* of different qualities in one person. In Beatrice, the poisonous angel of "Rappaccini's Daughter" (1844), he created such a complex heroine. . . .

. . . On the level of political activism, the late 1840s was the watershed moment when the Seneca Falls feminists initiated heated public agitation for women's rights.

Witnessing these swirling images of women in his contemporary culture, the observant Hawthorne brought them together in the figure of Hester Prynne. Given the cultural conditions and Hawthorne's personal experiences, it is understandable that he made a complex woman the center of his most famous novel. . . .

The Female Subversive

In *The Scarlet Letter* Hawthorne . . . takes the wholly original step of fashioning a heroine *who embodies all the dark female roles of the Subversive novel and who at the same time serves the redemptive function of the Conventional moral exemplar.* No character in antebellum fiction is so rich a compound of popular stereotypes as Hester Prynne. She is the sympathetically portrayed fallen woman whose honest sinfulness is found preferable to the furtive corruption of the reverend rake. She is the struggling working woman who plies her needle as a seamstress. She is the feminist criminal bound in an "iron link of mutual crime" with a man whose feebleness through most of the novel is contrasted with her indomitable firmness. She is the sensual woman who has, in Hawthorne's words, "a rich, voluptuous, Oriental characteristic" and who is bold enough to whisper to her lover, "What we did had a consecration of its own." She is the feminist exemplar who privately broods over women's wrongs and dreams of a revolution in relations between the sexes. She is all of these iconoclastic things—but she is also a moral exemplar, in both the angelic and the practical sense. She elicits from the Puritans "the reverence due to an angel," and one of the meanings associated with her letter is "Angel." Along with her angelic quality goes a practical ability to help others as a charity worker and an adviser.

She is, in short, the quintessential American heroine, reflecting virtually every facet of the antebellum woman's experience. . . .

We sympathize with Hester but, because of the enormity of her punishment (a punishment reflecting the moral severity of Puritan New England), we are impressed with the momentousness of her sin. That is to say, she is not the fallen woman of the antebellum sensational novel who becomes callously amoral or vindicatively murderous. Similarly, she is not the typical working woman, one who either gives way to suicidal despair, or becomes a prostitute, or contemplates armed revolution. Hawthorne knew well the plight of American seamstresses, and in the novel he points out that needlework was "then, as now, almost the only one within a woman's grasp." But instead of emphasizing the degradation accompanying woman's work, he transforms this work into a triumphant assertion of woman's artistic power, as evidenced by the intricate, superb patterns Hester produces. . . .

Feminist Leadership

The feminist exemplar is another popular stereotype Hawthorne transforms. At key points in the novel we are told that Hester broods over women's wrongs and dreams of a total change in male-female relations. But she never agitates publicly for women's rights, and it is clear by the end of the novel that Hawthorne has in mind not a militant, angry feminism but rather a gradualist moral exemplar feminism with utopian overtones. As a counselor of troubled women, the aged Hester assures them that "at some brighter period, when the world shall have grown ripe for it, in Heaven's own time, a new truth would be revealed, in order to establish the whole relation between man and woman on a surer ground of mutual happiness." Not only is the feminist revolution delayed to a vague, ideal future, but also Hester discounts her own capacities as a feminist exemplar by stressing that "the angel and apostle of the coming revelation must be a woman indeed, but lofty, pure and beautiful" and wise "not through dusky grief, but the ethereal medium of joy."

Hawthorne, therefore, attempts in *The Scarlet Letter* to absorb his culture's darkest, most disturbing female stereotypes and to rescue them from prurience or noisy politics by reinterpreting them in terms of bygone Puritanism and by fusing them with the moral exemplar.

A Mixture of Feminism and Misogyny

Alison Easton

Alison Easton is an honorary research fellow at Lancaster University, where she was previously Senior Lecturer in English and served as codirector of the university's Centre for Women's Studies (1991–1994). She is the author of The Making of the Hawthorne Subject *(1996) and editor of a Penguin collection of the works of Sarah Orne Jewett (1995).*

Alison Easton first puts the story of Hester Prynne in the context of changing social mores after the American Revolution. Many women, including Hawthorne's mother, were already pregnant when they married, but by the 1830s a stricter code was in place, and the differences between men's and women's places had become more rigid. In The Scarlet Letter, *Easton argues, Hawthorne expresses both misogynist and feminist views but never definitively sides with one or the other. Particularly revealing are Hester's two conversations with Chillingworth, her forest meeting with Dimmesdale, her irreverent musings, and her state of mind when she returns to Boston. The voice that judges her is puzzling and complicates what we are to understand as Hawthorne's view of Hester. But no careful reading can conclusively find her either completely radical or in total submissive atonement.*

In 1802, less than thirty-one weeks after her wedding, Elizabeth Manning Hawthorne gave birth to her first child, Elizabeth. Nathaniel Hawthorne the writer, her second child, was born two years later. Interestingly, there are only two things we can say with certainty about this bridal pregnancy. First, we do not know how Hawthorne's parents, their families or

Alison Easton, *The Cambridge Companion to Nathaniel Hawthorne*. New York: Cambridge University Press, 2004.

indeed Hawthorne himself regarded it. Second, the reason that we cannot infer their responses is that, while one in three brides were pregnant in the last third of the eighteenth century, by 1850 when Hawthorne published *The Scarlet Letter* bridal pregnancies had become infrequent and completely unacceptable. . . .

Mid-Nineteenth-Century Ideology

This is one of those historical moments that remind us that patriarchal structures do not remain constant, and the sites of tension change. Class formation too is a crucial factor. Post-Revolution family structures and values gradually but significantly altered, placing new emphasis on a love-relationship between husband and wife and on nurturing self-governance in children, and rather less on wider kin and community relations. There was an accompanying shift away from traditional categorizing of women in terms of subservience, weakness, and inferiority toward a notion of the tender female "heart"; women's social dependency was reconstructed as a female concern for others. So, while women might want the same increased opportunities as men and indeed some did paid work in the burgeoning capitalist economy until the late 1830s, new sex role distinctions were firmly in place by the end of the eighteenth century that would eventually pin most married white women and unmarried middle-class women to the home. In the late 1830s the middle-class home emerged, reimagined as a private sanctuary from the world of money-making.

So, powerful ideological images came to dominate bourgeois women's lives and thinking about women mid-century. Nonetheless, Hawthorne was in his thirties before this view of marriage became dominant, and even when well established, it was never a wholly shared, coherent, or simple vision socially. There was bound to be a gap between lived experiences, and the bourgeois ideology of "True Womanhood," that is to say a pious, asexual, submissive, domestic femininity. Women also knew the importance of self-reliance, hard work, orderliness, and practical skills. Nor were they "passionless"; rather, the evidence is that sexual experience was highly valued but extremely private. While fervid attempts were made to close the gap between ideology and experience, Hawthorne was to explore the multiple implications of this socially constructed doubleness. . . .

Although ideological efforts were made to contain the question of women through the concept or separate gendered "spheres" of existence, men's and women's lives were, of course, inextricably intertwined; only in ideology were women and domesticity totally aligned to the exclusion of the public. Margaret Fuller, the greatest feminist thinker of mid-century America, based her analysis, *Woman in the Nineteenth Century* (1845), on this understanding that women were not insulated from the public realm, nor were men detached from the domestic, but that all inhabited a common world, albeit differently. There was no way that Hawthorne could have been unaffected. . . .

The Uncertainty of Hawthorne's View

There is evidence of both feminist and misogynist views in his imaginative and non-fictional writings which have been hotly debated, but there simply is no certainty about what he believed, and we should be wary when his texts make apparently definitive pronouncements. . . . It is undeniably tempting for twenty-first century critics to construct Hawthorne in our own image, but to read his works as simply feminist or misogynist—as presently defined—we would have to ignore a great deal. . . .

Likewise, Hawthorne's modern readers will find him ahead of us in the work of identifying his society's dreams and contradictions about women. He thematizes its problems, quotes its formulations so that we hear them freshly, and dramatizes its conflicts, while his sense of historical change in the way men and women live modifies his own and his culture's attachment to the idea of an unchanging female "nature." . . .

A Feminist Conversation

At the end of *The Scarlet Letter*, "Women, more especially,—in the continually recurring trials of wounded, wasted, wronged, misplaced, or erring and sinful passion,—or with the dreary burden of a heart unyielded, because unvalued and unsought,—came to Hester's cottage, demanding why they were so wretched, and what the remedy!" The red A's original religious and judicial "office" (that is, function) has startlingly metamorphosed into a feminist conversation. Paradoxically, in this post-adultery novel, marriage is central, as indeed it was for most nineteenth-century women's lives (nearly 90 percent married). While the novel of adultery is one standard way to explore marriage, *The Scarlet Letter*'s unusual concern exclusively with the deed's denouement gives sustained attention to a figure encountered earlier, the "unhoused" woman; the once married woman reveals female subjectivity more fully in separation. In addition, as Fuller had noted in *Woman in the Nineteenth Century*, it is the unattached woman who tests many common gender assumptions. . . .

Indeed, the dismissal of Hester's story in "The Custom-House" as "proving of no public concern" invites the opposite judgment. Strikingly, the novel touches on so much of nineteenth-century female experience highlighted by contemporary feminist analyses as requiring public recognition and social reform: marriage, domestic abuse, divorce, child-rearing, and child custody, working women (including seamstresses), political exclusion, and, crucially for our purposes, "fallen" women condemned for their sexual history (a highly public topic).

The novel returns to "The Gentle Boy" topic of a woman publicly at odds with the state; this time, the initiating concern is with sexuality, intimacy, and secrecy, the mother does not abandon her child, nor is the child "gentle." With a "dead woman's features" in public, Hester is one of Hawthorne's wives of the dead, but with redoubled complexity. Three extraordinary conversations open up a dissenting discussion on marriage: with Chillingworth in prison and again seven years later on the seashore, and the forest meeting with Dimmesdale. Notably, Hawthorne's first audiences found this material disquieting in ways that most twenty-first century readers, in Western society grown accustomed to divorce, are unlikely to do. Whereas "highly respectable" spectators of the final scaffold scene subsequently censor their memories, these explicit conversations are impossible for the reader to ignore.

With profound subversion the early prison encounter perversely enacts a domestic, family scene—sick child tended in the doctor's arms, intimate conversation of husband and wife. Whereas on the theocratic scaffold Hester is unambiguously guilty, the private discussion redefines the rights and wrongs of marriage in emotional and sexual terms that condemn both parties to that loveless contract. [Her] betrayed husband startlingly announces, "We have wronged each other." The novel is still taking marriage very seriously, but here its "intimate and sacred" quality makes demands irrelevant to the Mosaic code. By the time Hester continues this conversation seven years later at the settlement's edge, she has evolved an even more radical position that swings from agonized responsibility for Chillingworth's psychological destruction to revulsion (triggered by ugly sexual memories) at his "fouler offence."

A View of Marriage

Despite *The Scarlet Letter*'s historical sense in other matters, these two scenes anachronistically dramatize nineteenth-century issues which were the inevitable outcome of the shift toward a concept of marriage based on love choice, intimacy, and mutual consideration. Whereas bridal pregnancies, such as Hawthorne's mother's, had been an earlier, benign aspect of this change, now the inevitable gap between new expectations and actualities produced, on the one hand, a conservative gender ideology touting wifely submissiveness to keep the lid on the ideas Hester expresses, and, on the other hand, feminist attempts to conceptualize a good marriage (Fuller, for example, lists different kinds of marriage in *Woman in the Nineteenth Century*). This new view of marriage also disturbingly underlies Hester's avowal to Dimmesdale that, "What we did had a consecration of its own. We felt it so! We said so to each other!"

Simultaneously, in the face of troubling outcomes of past decisions, Hester finds herself evolving an additional, and eventually alternative, discourse of responsibility to her former lover which, again, would have been disturbing to the novel's earliest readers since she is "connected in a union . . . unrecognized on earth": to admit Chillingworth's continued existence with, "'he *was* my husband,'" must seem immensely challenging. The phrase, "wives of the dead," here takes on immense complexities. It is not a simple matter of substituting one set of obligations for another; indeed, although Hester finally works out a morality that justifies doing this, the novel's climax suggests its impossibility.

So, the novel cannot be read in approving sympathy for doomed lovers (nor, for that matter, disapproval). The novel stays open, pushing the reader simultaneously or sequentially toward seemingly opposing views, or rather toward the recognition that it cannot be a matter of one view or another but rather an inextricable web of relationships that creates complex subjects. This is achieved partly by means of a narrator who struggles with confusion even while censuring Hester's dissidence. Slippery syntax also keeps the reader uncertain about narrative focalization—that is, whether we are being shown a character's subjective view or whether these statements have some kind of external authority. . . .

The Role of Pearl

In the role of wild child, Pearl evinces an innocent curiosity about meeting the "Black Man": she is gentle in the forest, but like the animals there reacts fiercely in defence. Thus she complicates the question of women's "nature" in a novel that repeatedly assumes knowledge of, or speculates upon, supposedly innate female qualities. The novel asks, "That unsunned snow in the matron's bosom, and the burning shame on Hester Prynne's,—what had the two in common?", and in answer suggests a "sisterhood"—not a co-operative relationship since the townswomen are patently hostile at first, but the possibility that the common distinction between "virgin" and the "fallen" occludes elements in common. On this basis Hester is exemplary of other women's potential, and her final role as counselor is therefore comprehensible and powerful. Moreover, her speculation on the question of women brilliantly blurs the distinction between nature and culture: "As a first step, the whole system of society is to be torn down, and built up anew. Then, the very nature of the opposite sex, or its long hereditary habit, which has become like nature, is to be essentially modified, before woman can be allowed to assume what seems a fair and suitable position."

Most significantly, the equation of "wild" with "fallen" is disrupted in Pearl whose green seaweed letter mirrors her mother's A (she must after all engage with social signification), yet promises uncensored passion, creative growth, and a fresh start (Pearl disappears finally into some "unknown region"). In the wonderful seaweed letter scene Pearl's insistent questioning of the scarlet letter's meaning (plus imagining her mother's questioning of the green A) further opens possibilities, and suggests more than child's play. The adult "noble woman" that Hester then glimpses in the child offers an image of apparently innate femininity very different from mid nineteenth-century gender conventions, but nonetheless conversant with other qualities recognizable from women's actual lives and indeed celebrated by Fuller: "the stedfast principles of an unflinching courage,—an uncontrollable will,—a sturdy pride, which might be disciplined into self-respect,—and a bitter scorn of many things, which, when examined, might be found to have the taint of falsehood in them." Not knowing how this new femininity will be expressed, Hester is scared into a harsh and surprisingly conservative response: she censors Pearl's discussion, substitutes a stereotypical image of feminine vanity for the letter's meaning and threatens the "naughty" daughter punitively with a "dark closet." Hester's subversion and submission turn out to be fearsomely interconnected, but Pearl suggests true difference.

One must then ask whether this aborted moment of sympathy between mother and daughter is recuperated in the final scaffold scene which "developed all [Pearl's] sympathies." "Tenderness," a recurring term in the novel, is central here. It is deemed particularly "feminine," and associated with natural impressionableness, ready sensitivity, demonstrative affection, considerate compassion, ready forgiveness, and support. It is not mere softness; it involves strength and passion, including the erotic, and the loving male is capable of it too. The longing for such tenderness started that seaweed letter exchange; indeed, from a nineteenth-century viewpoint the emotional structure of tenderness derives primarily from the mother/child relationship (something on which Dimmesdale himself relies as he finally totters, childlike, to the scaffold). As Fuller remarked, "All the secret powers are 'Mothers.' There is but one paternal power." So while the narrator, with decidedly conservative views on women, fixes Pearl's tears into a "softened and subdued" womanhood, the qualities that they signal suggest a more passionate and transformative femininity. However, although Fuller envisaged a feminist revolution—"And will not she soon appear? The woman who shall vindicate their birthright for all women; who shall teach them what to claim, and how to use what they obtain"—Hawthorne's novel severely qualifies this in suggesting that "the angel and apostle of the coming revelation" can only be a happy woman.

Puritans and Feminists

Leland S. Person

Leland S. Person, professor of English at the University of Cincinnati, is the author of Aesthetic Headaches *(1988),* Henry James and the Suspense of Masculinity *(2003), and* A Historical Guide to James Fenimore Cooper *(2007).*

Hawthorne, a political and social conservative, was fully exposed to advocates for women's rights after he and Sophia moved to Concord, Massachusetts. Not only were the men he encountered in favor of reforms for women, but also, his close friend Margaret Fuller voiced one of the earliest protests against the abasement of women. In the following viewpoint, Person notes that critics have seen Hester's forest meeting with Dimmesdale (when she voices her conviction that their adultery had a consecration of its own) as issuing from his walks with Fuller. Leland S. Person contends that, like Fuller and Hester, Hawthorne was furious at the old Puritan oligarchy, who had fired him from his job at the Salem Custom House just before he wrote The Scarlet Letter. *Hawthorne has his heroine break the rules of female submission by elaborately decorating her badge of shame, conducting herself proudly, and refusing to allow those in power to remove her child from her (as nineteenth-century divorced men could legally do). Hester's historical connections to the Puritans and the nineteenth-century reformists highlight her feminism and her belief that the whole fabric of society must be changed for woman to have equality, opportunity, independence, and a voice.*

[After leaving the utopian community of Brook Farm in 1841], Hawthorne embarked upon several publishing projects, including the second edition of *Twice-Told Tales* and

Leland S. Person, *The Cambridge Introduction to Nathaniel Hawthorne*. New York: Cambridge University Press, 2007.

Biographical Stories for Children, while he planned for his marriage to Sophia. He arranged with [Transcendentalist thinker Ralph Waldo] Emerson to rent his family's Old Manse in Concord, and he and Sophia moved in on their wedding day (9 July 1842). Situated on the banks of the Concord River and overlooking the site of the Old North Bridge and the first battleground of the Revolutionary War, the Old Manse stimulated Hawthorne's imagination. The three years he spent in Concord (July 1842-November 1845) represent a fascinating period in his life. Concord in the 1840s was a kind of intellectual utopian community and included a remarkable gathering of intellectual and artistic personalities: Emerson, [Henry David] Thoreau, Margaret Fuller, Bronson Alcott, Ellery Channing, and others whom we now associate with the Transcendentalist, abolitionist, women's suffrage, and other reform movements. These friendships have provided Hawthorne's modern readers with much food for speculation about influence, rivalry, and cross-pollination. Hawthorne's notebooks record numerous visits and outings that, if time travel were a possibility, literary scholars would pay dearly to observe. . . .

The Radical Woman

In *Hawthorne's Fuller Mystery*, Thomas Mitchell has carefully analyzed Hawthorne's relationship with Margaret Fuller, and he details the times they spent together during the Concord years. Mitchell argues for Fuller's profound influence on Hawthorne and his writing, especially on such characters as Beatrice Rappaccini, Hester Prynne, Zenobia in *The Blithedale Romance*, and Miriam Schaefer in *The Marble Faun*. Hawthorne's letters and notebooks record many visits that Fuller paid to the Old Manse, and he described one remarkable meeting with Fuller in a lengthy notebook entry for 22 August 1842. Fuller was staying with the Emersons, and Hawthorne set out after dinner to return a book she had left at the Manse. Fuller was not home when he called, but he encountered her on his return journey through the woods in Sleepy Hollow. Sitting by Margaret's side, Hawthorne would note, "we talked about Autumn—and about the pleasures of getting lost in the woods—and about the crows, whose voices Margaret had heard . . . and about the sight of mountains from a distance, and the view from their summits—and about other matters of high and low philosophy." As Mitchell has argued, this scene and passage may provide a basis for the forest scene in *The Scarlet Letter* in which Hester Prynne and Arthur Dimmesdale make their plans to leave Boston. Hester famously declares, "What we did had a consecration of its own. We felt it so! We said so to each other!" . . .

Financial Struggles

Hawthorne left the Old Manse and Concord because he could not afford to live there. Magazine publication paid poorly, and the Hawthornes struggled to pay rent on the Old Manse, especially after [their daughter] Una's birth. Friends such as Franklin Pierce, Horatio Bridge, and John O'Sullivan tried to help by finding Hawthorne another government job. The only option Hawthorne could imagine was to return home—to Salem and the Manning House [Sophia's parents' home]. Five months later, he finally secured a lucrative political appointment from President James K. Polk as Surveyor of the Salem Custom House. His yearly earnings approached $1,200. He must have breathed a huge sigh of relief. . . .

Hawthorne kept his position as Surveyor for three years, until election of the Whig Zachary Taylor to the Presidency resulted in his firing in the summer of 1849. Hawthorne and his friends tried unsuccessfully to retain the Surveyor's position amid increasingly politicized accusations of corruption. Hawthorne protested that he had not been "appointed to office as a reward for political services," nor had he "acted as a politician since," and he vowed to "immolate" his critics if they should succeed in getting him out of office. . . .

Anger Against the Oligarchy

He would have his revenge on his political enemies in *The Scarlet Letter*, the novel he sat down to write almost immediately after he lost his job as Surveyor. He would tell his publisher, James T. Fields, that in the process of writing, "all political and official turmoil has subsided within me, so that I have not felt inclined to execute justice on any of my enemies," but most scholars think Hawthorne merely sublimated his anger in his depiction of the Puritans who, though actually members of the Massachusetts Bay colony, stand in for the Salemites with whom Hawthorne felt angry. Many readers have seen a connection between Hawthorne and his heroine, whose punishment and ostracism from the Puritan community force her to eke out a living as a kind of artist....

Puritanism

Despite Hawthorne's reputation as a romancer who preferred to create a "neutral territory, somewhere between the real world and fairy-land" and seemed intent upon liberating his tales and novels from the everyday world, he paid careful attention to historical settings for most of his literary works. He conducted his research, often reading extensively in historical sources, but he routinely changed facts to suit his imaginative purpose. He often sought historical distance as a way of dealing with volatile contemporary issues, such as slavery or women's rights. Regardless of a work's situation in history, however, readers must deal with a tension between historical moments. *The Scarlet Letter* offers the best case in point. Set in Puritan Boston between 1642 and 1649 (the years of the English Civil War), the novel owes a great deal to seventeenth-century sources, but the most interesting recent research has emphasized the book's treatment of nineteenth-century issues. A key challenge for readers often means figuring out how Hawthorne's use of early history helps him deal with more contemporary matters.

Puritanism and the history of early Massachusetts settlements—Massachusetts Bay, Plymouth, and Salem—form one important context in which to understand Hawthorne's writing. Hawthorne read widely in seventeenth-century history, both English and American. Scholars such as Charles Ryskamp and Michael Colacurcio have meticulously connected characters and events in *The Scarlet Letter* and other works to the New England historical record. *The Journal of John Winthrop* and Winthrop's *The History of New England from 1630 to 1649* (1825–26), Caleb H. Snow's *A History of Boston* (1825), and Joseph Felt's *The Annals of Salem from Its First Settlement* (1827) represent especially important sources from which Hawthorne took background information. He also drew upon aspects of his personal history. In both "Young Goodman Brown" and *The Scarlet Letter*, he refers to his earliest American ancestors. Hawthorne's great-great-great grandfather, William Hathorne, was a notable public figure in Salem after he settled there in 1636, serving on the Board of Selectmen for many years and fighting in King Philip's War. At one point, he ordered a Quaker woman, Ann Coleman, to be whipped through the streets of Salem. John Hathorne, William's son, presided at the Salem witch trials in 1692. In "The Custom-House," the preface he wrote to *The Scarlet Letter*, Hawthorne referred to each of these ancestors as a "bitter persecutor" who possessed "all the Puritanic traits, both good and evil." Hawthorne felt haunted by these ancestors and took shame upon himself "for their sakes," hoping that *The Scarlet Letter* would cause "any curse incurred by them" to be "now and henceforth removed."

Hawthorne's portrait of the Puritans, especially in *The Scarlet Letter*, has probably influenced our impression of Puritanism more than any other literary work, with the possible exception of Arthur Miller's treatment of the Salem witch trials in *The Crucible* (1952). That is, we associate Puritanism with superstition, excessive moralism, intolerance, and patriarchal oppression. . . .

Intolerance of Women

The key controversy in early Puritan New England—the Antinomian controversy of 1636–38—involved charges by Anne Hutchinson that most ministers in the Massachusetts Bay Colony were preaching a "Covenant of Works" rather than a "Covenant of Grace." By this term, David Hall explains, "she meant that the ministers were letting people 'thinke [themselves] to be saved, because they see some worke of Sanctification in them.'" For Hutchinson individual behavior played no role in salvation, but she also based her ministry on a "personal sense of communion with the Holy Spirit" and so "could deny that the ministry was needed as an intervening 'means of grace' between God and man." For making charges against other ministers (all of them men) and for hosting religious services for women in her home, Hutchinson was banished to Rhode Island in 1638. . . .

Puritan beliefs lay behind the Salem witchcraft hysteria of 1692, in which twenty people from Salem Village (now Danvers, Massachusetts) were executed for practicing witchcraft on their neighbors. . . .

Hester Prynne has historical sources, too, but American rather than English. In his *History of New England*, John Winthrop notes that Mary Latham of Plymouth Colony and James Britton were condemned to die for adultery in March 1644. Winthrop explains that Mary Latham had been rejected by a young man she loved, vowed to marry the "next that came to her," and ended up "matched with an ancient man" for whom she had no affection. Hawthorne also knew the case of Salem's Hester Craford, who in 1688 was ordered to be "severely whipped" for fornication with John Wedg. The judgment, which was carried out by William Hathorne, was suspended for a month so that this Hester could give birth to the child she and Wedg had conceived.

An earlier and more important antecedent is Anne Hutchinson, who was banished from Massachusetts for unlawful

Margaret Fuller, an American writer and a close friend of Nathaniel Hawthorne, voiced one of the earliest protests against the abasement of women. Hulton Archive/Getty Images.

preaching and, in Governor John Winthrop's words, for "being a woman not fit for our society." Hawthorne had devoted one of his earliest sketches, "Mrs. Hutchinson" (1830), to her experiences. In the first chapter of the novel Hawthorne observes that a rose bush grows by the prison door—a rose bush that had "sprung up under the foot of the sainted Ann Hutchinson." Hutchinson was charged with unlawfully hosting weekly meetings for women—behavior, in Winthrop's terms, not "fitting for your sex." The Puritans' objections to Hutchinson involved her interpretation of scripture, but the magistrates' comments also suggest that they resented having a woman doing that heretical preaching. In the very middle of *The Scarlet Letter* (chapter 13) Hawthorne explicitly compares Hester Prynne to Hutchinson—as a woman and a radical. If Hester had not had Pearl to keep her rooted in her family responsibilities, he says, "she might have come down to us in history, hand in hand with Ann Hutchinson, as the foundress of a religious sect. She might . . . have been a prophetess." By which he seems to mean a feminist, for he goes on to suggest, in terms that resonate more for nineteenth-century readers than they would have for his seventeenth-century characters, that Hester might have sponsored a movement in which the "whole system of society is to be torn down, and built up anew" so that women "can be allowed to assume what seems a fair and suitable position." . . .

Hester and the Struggle for Rights

Hawthorne wrote during a period of political turmoil, especially because of the human rights movements that characterize the middle of the nineteenth century. . . .

In 1837, the year that Hawthorne published *Twice-Told Tales*, Mary Lyon opened Mount Holyoke Female Seminary (now Mount Holyoke College), the first institution founded to provide higher education to women. Many abolitionists argued in behalf of women's rights—for example, Lydia Maria Child in her *History of the Condition of Women* (1835), Sarah Grimké in *Letters on the Equality of the Sexes* (1838), and especially Margaret Fuller in "The Great Lawsuit" (1843) and *Woman in the Nineteenth Century*, which she published in 1845, the year before Hawthorne published *Mosses from an Old Manse*.

Hawthorne seemed minimally affected by these movements, and it was common in criticism before the last twenty years to situate his writing within a romance tradition in which "real world" concerns had only a faint presence. More recent scholars have found plenty of evidence that Hawthorne's writing bears traces of the cultural moment out of which he wrote. By the time he published *The Scarlet Letter*, for example, Hawthorne knew Fuller very well. The first major women's rights convention, held in July of 1848 in Seneca Falls, New York, occurred just a year before he sat down to begin the novel about a woman who rebels against patriarchal authority. Despite the distant setting, it is hard to imagine *The Scarlet Letter* not entering into a conversation with nineteenth-century feminism.

Recent scholarship on Hawthorne's writing in a context formed by women, women's issues, and women's writing, has come a long way from the character typology approaches of earlier periods. Along with James Fenimore Cooper, Edgar Allan Poe, Melville, and others, Hawthorne comes to mind when we think of nineteenth-century female stereotypes, especially the familiar opposition of Fair Maidens and Dark Ladies. . . .

Hawthorne understood the power of radical women, and in Hester Prynne, as in Anne Hutchinson, he created a heroine who is as much a nineteenth-century feminist as a seventeenth-century Puritan heretic. Zenobia in *The Blithedale Romance* is more obviously patterned after Margaret Fuller. Thomas Mitchell finds Fuller's influence pervasive, and *The Scarlet Letter* includes several passages that seem to echo lines in Fuller's ground-breaking feminist book, *Woman in the Nineteenth Century*. At the end of *The Scarlet Letter*, for example, Hester assures the women who come to her cottage of "her firm belief, that, at some brighter period, when the world should have grown ripe for it, in Heaven's own time, a new truth would be revealed, in order to establish the whole relation between man and woman on a surer ground of mutual happiness." When Fuller comments on the prospects for feminist reform, she writes, "then and only then will mankind be ripe for this, when inward and outward freedom for Woman as much as for Man shall be acknowledged as a *right*, not yielded as a concession." The unusual word "ripe" stands out in each passage; Hawthorne's use of the word in a sentence that echoes Fuller's in other respects as well suggests that he was borrowing from Fuller. Both writers look forward to a time when American society will be "ripe" for the growth of real women, and both find it very difficult to specify that time. . . .

Despite his disparagement of most women writers, Hawthorne populated his fiction with many powerful female artists. Hester Prynne is not a writer, except in the loosest sense, but she is an artist, and she comes before the public, in a sense, "stark naked." She embroiders the scarlet letter as if the Devil were in her before displaying it to the public for the first time and so asserts some power over the letter as a signifier. For the rest of the novel, her artistry seems confined to the domestic sphere, although even there it is not without its subversive power.

Hester as Hero

Nina Baym

Professor emerita of English at the University of Illinois at Urbana-Champaign, Nina Baym has authored and edited many books, including American Women of Letters and the Nineteenth-Century Sciences *(2002),* Feminism and American Literary History *(1992), and* The Shape of Hawthorne's Career *(1976).*

In the following selection Nina Baym asserts that Hester's actions and strengths reveal her to be a true hero. Her power is shown, early on, in her decision to remain in Boston. The letter she wears never changes her inwardly, as is evident from her radical musings and her forest conversation with Dimmesdale. It is her love of Pearl that reins her in and keeps her from witchcraft and open reformism. By embellishing the A *she is forced to wear, Hester controls her own way of life, in defiance of the Puritans. She practices her calling as an artist through the only means available to her—as a seamstress. In this way, the society of Puritans appropriate her art for their own purposes, as luxurious apparel that only those of high social standing are allowed to wear. The* A*, once standing for "adultery," is, at the end, interpreted by many people as "able."*

In Hester Prynne, Hawthorne created the first true heroine of American fiction, as well as one of its enduring heroes. Hester is a heroine because she is deeply implicated in, and responsive to, the gender structure of her society, and because her story, turning on "love," is "appropriate" for a woman. She is a hero because she has qualities and actions that transcend this gender reference and lead to heroism as it can be understood for anyone.

Nina Baym, *The Scarlet Letter: A Reading*. Belmont, CA: Twayne Publishers, 1986.

Good Power

"Such helpfulness was found in her,—so much power to do, and power to sympathize,—that many people refused to interpret the scarlet *A* by its original signification. They said that it meant Able; so strong was Hester Prynne, with a woman's strength." "Neither can I any longer live without her companionship; so powerful is she to sustain,—so tender to soothe!" It is impossible to miss, in these and many other passages, the stress on Hester's remarkable strength as well as the fundamentally humane uses to which she puts it. Without going beyond the license that Hawthorne allows, one might allegorize Hester as Good Power, which is, after all, precisely what, in the basic structural scheme of all narrative, one looks for in a hero. The power is remarkable in that its existence seems so improbable in an outcast woman. If the Puritan state draws its power from the consensual community and the laws that uphold it, then clearly Hester has access to a completely different source of power—or is, perhaps, herself an alternative source of power. And it is a power that even the Puritan world cannot deny, for "with her native energy of character, and rare capacity, it could not entirely cast her off."

Perhaps, however, it is precisely her essential alienation from the community that explains this power. Although Hester can hardly doubt the power of the Puritan community to punish her and define the circumstances of her life, she knows—as we do—that they have this power only because she has granted it to them. She is free to leave Boston whenever she chooses. Her decision to stay entails a submission to Puritan power, but since she can withdraw her consent at any time this submission is always provisional. Her reasons for staying may be misguided, but they are her own. In schematic terms, if the Puritans symbolize the law, then Hester symbolizes the individual person—with this important proviso: she also symbolizes good. It would be easy to deduce from this polarity that Hawthorne wants us to think that law is bad and the individual good—but that would be too easy. Matters in Hawthorne are never so clear-cut. But he certainly gives us a situation wherein two kinds of power confront each other in conflict, and strongly suggests that any society that regards the power of the individual only as an adversary to be overcome, is profoundly defective and deeply inhuman.

Hester's situation, even before the commission of her "sin," is that of an outsider. She was sent to Massachusetts in advance of her husband; he has decided to emigrate, not she. The native strength of her character is certainly abetted by the fact that, as a young woman in a society dominated by aging men, she has no public importance. Even when she becomes a public figure through her punishment, her psyche is largely left alone. The magistrates condemn her to wear the letter but thereafter seem to have only a very superficial interest in her. A minister who sees her on the street may take the opportunity to preach an extempore sermon; people stare at the letter; children jeer; but none of this behavior represents an attempt to change Hester's mind. It is hoped that the external letter will work its way down into Hester's heart and cause repentance, but nobody really cares and this indifference is Hester's freedom. In fact, the effect of the letter so far as Hester's character is concerned is the opposite of what was intended: turning her into a public symbol, it conceals her individuality and thus protects it.

Hester and the Law

As the representative of individuality, Hester, rather than subjecting herself to the law, subjects it to her own scrutiny; as I have said, she takes herself as a law. She is not, by nature, rebellious; and during the seven-year period of *The Scarlet Letter*'s action, she certainly attempts to accept the judgment implicit in the letter. If she could accept that judgment she would be able to see purpose and meaning in her suffering. But ultimately she is unable to transcend her heartfelt conviction that she has not sinned. She loves Dimmesdale, with whom she sinned; she loves the child that her sin brought forth. How, then, can she agree that her deed was wrong?

She goes so far in her thinking as to attribute her own law to God, thus denying the entire rationale of the Puritan community, their certainty that their laws conform to divine intention. "Man had marked this woman's sin by a scarlet letter, which had such potent and disastrous efficacy that no human sympathy could reach her, save it were sinful like herself. God, as a direct consequence of the sin which man thus punished, had given her a lovely child, whose place was on that same dishonored bosom, to connect her parent for ever with the race and descent of mortals, and to be finally a blessed soul in heaven!"

In fact, while the outward Hester performs deeds of mercy and kindness throughout the seven years, the inward Hester grows ever more alienated and over time becomes—what she was not at first—a genuine revolutionary and social radical. . . .

Pearl Tempers Hester's Rebellion

Had she spoken her thoughts, she probably would "have suffered death from the stern tribunals of the period, for attempting to undermine the foundations of the Puritan establishment." If it were not for the existence of Pearl, for whose sake she lives quietly in Boston, she would have become, like Anne Hutchinson, a religious reformer.

But just as Hester refuses to take the road to witchcraft on account of Pearl, she rejects Hutchinson's radical path for the same reason. She feels particular obligations to human beings far more than she feels general social responsibilities. She behaves as a sister of mercy in the community because this is the way to live unmolested, not because she believes in doing good. And she wants to live unmolested so that she can bring up Pearl. Staying in Boston on account of Dimmesdale, and living there as she does on account of Pearl, Hester's behavior is appropriate to her role as representative of individual and personal, rather than social, power. A reformer is dedicated to social power and has abandoned an individual center. No doubt this makes the whole issue of social reform on behalf of individualism highly problematic; so far as Hester is concerned—and this is our concern at present—the very consistency of her individualism keeps her within the sphere of the personal. At the end of the story, with her group of women clustered about her, she invokes the memory of Hutchinson only to contrast with it. The subject of talk among the women is entirely personal, centered on secular love; Hester counsels patience. Thus, the narrator's suggestion that her radicalism stems from an unquiet heart is partly validated by her behavior. If in Hawthorne's world a true radical, motivated by the impersonal, is somehow anti-individual, and if a true individual, motivated by the personal, is ultimately not radical, then our current popular understanding of these terms is quite different from Hawthorne's. His distinction is between ideologues and individuals rather than between varieties of ideology: an "individual-ist" is an ideologue. The individual as a reality rather than a concept is always extremely vulnerable.

An Artistic Nature

Among Hester's key defining traits we cannot overlook her "skill at her needle." If her nature includes the characters of outcast, rebel, lover, mother, and sister of mercy, it also includes the character of artist. Her gift for needlework is the expression of an artist's nature; the embroideries that she produces are genuine works of art.

We meet her skill first, of course, in the letter, which, "surrounded with an elaborate embroidery and fantastic flourishes of gold thread," is "so artistically done, and with so much fertility and gorgeous luxuriance of fancy, that it had all the effect of a last and fitting decoration" to her splendid apparel. Hester's grand costuming for the scaffold scene, far more elegant than what the dress code of the colony normally would allow her, is not seen again. She wears nothing but drab gray gowns. Her dreary dress, however, becomes a frame for the letter, and the letter remains, as it is clearly meant to be, an ornament. Beautifying the letter through art is another way in which Hester breaks the Puritan law (although the Puritan rulers—unlike the women in the crowd—are too literal-minded to notice it). The letter becomes the chief ground for the struggle between Hester and the Puritans, and it is able to play this role because of Hester's gift as an artist.

It is tempting here to associate artistic skill with social rebellion, but the equation does not hold. For Hester supports herself in Puritan Boston chiefly by making the elaborate decorative garments that the magistrates wear for public occasions and that are allowed to the better-off in the colony. "Deep ruffs, painfully wrought bands, and gorgeously embroidered gloves, were all deemed necessary to the official state of men assuming the reins of power; and were readily allowed to individuals dignified by rank or wealth." Art does not have an inherently political nature, although—as the instance of the letter shows—it can become highly politicized. Rather, it is the expression of an original and creative energy, of fertility, of imagination, and of the love for the beautiful, even the gorgeous. This energy and creativity have no reference to society at all. Artists and their products can be appropriated by society or condemned by it; but society cannot make art, only individuals can. Indeed, only individuals who retain, or contain, a profound nonsocial element in their makeup (as Hester does) can make art. Although the social structure of the age denies virtually all forms of artistic expression to women, it does allow this one, and Hester makes use of it as an outlet for this side of her nature. For its part, society makes use of *her*. The Puritans may be incapable of producing art, but they certainly want to possess it. Therefore, despite everything, they want Hester in their community; and they want her *as she is.*

But this is something they have to learn about themselves; and if they do not learn in time, there will be a society with no more Hesters.

Woman Identified with the Marginalized Artist

Ken Egan Jr.

Professor of English and department chair at Drury University, Ken Egan Jr. is the author of Hope and Dread in Montana Literature *(2003),* The Riven Home: Narrative Rivalry in the American Renaissance *(1997), and numerous articles on nineteenth-century literature.*

Ken Egan Jr. argues that there is a close identification between Hawthorne's view of his own literary art and Hester's adultery. The actions of both author and female protagonist are subversive in the eyes of society, and art (identified with adultery) is condemned by nineteenth-century society as salacious. When Hawthorne, an author, must enter the marketplace (that is, take a job at the Custom House) to support his family, he is belittled as an effeminate outsider. When Hester enters the marketplace, she is punished and, later, isolated. In order to survive, both must make compromises to appease society.

Rather than celebrating a communal victory over Satan and sinfulness, "The Custom-House" [the autobiographical sketch that serves as an introduction to *The Scarlet Letter*] employs a form of Puritan discourse to celebrate the individual artist's prevailing over oppression.

Art and artistry are crucial to the novel as well. Joel Porte has put the case most succinctly when he writes, "*The Scarlet Letter*, in short, can be read as an allegory of art." Porte calls our attention to Hawthorne's struggle to justify romantic art in a culture dominated by pragmatic concerns. Not surpris-

Ken Egan Jr., "The Adulteress in the Market-Place," *Studies in the Novel*, vol. xxvii, Spring 1995, pp. 26–28, 31–37.

ingly, then, we have focused on correspondences between the writer of the text and his artistic rebel, Hester Prynne. Both Hawthorne and Hester can be seen as subversive artists who must enter "the market-place" with a scarlet letter, signifier of pride and shame, achievement and alienation. However, we have not paid sufficient attention to role of adultery in this "allegory of art." Though Hester's "sin" is never openly announced, the text cleverly alludes to adultery and "adulteration" throughout, creating a kind of fetishistic fascination with the "nameless" crime. Granting that the novel and its prefatory sketch are concerned with the artist's role in antebellum America, the reader can fairly ask, "in what sense is artistic reproduction an act of adultery?" But I want to push this issue even farther by insisting on the question, "in what sense is the male author an adulteress?" Put in these terms, the issue resonates with concerns about Hawthorne's attitude toward women in general and female writers specifically. I will argue that, for Hawthorne, to be a male writer in his culture was necessarily to be an "adulteress," that is, a feminized adulterer of "the truth." Furthermore, his status as "adulteress" virtually required him to enter "the marketplace" of literature, for his transgressions of gender role and vocation forced him out of the paternalistic "house of custom" into the masculinist market. That is, having violated the expectations of a cultural son, the hermaphroditic writer must compete in the acquisitive, rowdy capitalist economy of antebellum America. Thus, the figure of the adulteress serves as a nexus for complex issues of vocation and gender Hawthorne had to confront at the moment of composing his novel and sketch. . . .

The Artist and the Woman on the Margin

Hester is indeed a kind of "liminal" character, caught betwixt and between social roles as a result of her passionate transgression. That liminality is emblemized by her virtual marginality, her abode located in the border region between city and forest, between the urban and the wild. Furthermore, as she attempts to fulfill her roles as mother and mate following the adulterous act and its issue, Hester struggles to meet the social demands of those roles. Her psychological traumas largely result from her confused desire to fulfill socially defined obligations while at the same time living on the margins of those obligations. Put differently, Hester attempts to be a "good" wife and mother while living out the legacy of her social disgrace. . . .

Like Hester, the male writer must dwell among multiple, conflicting personae while somehow making a living and maintaining an imaginative integrity. A father, a husband, a son, a worker, Hawthorne must yet acknowledge his "feminine" qualities, those qualities associated with his "authorship." . . .

Authoring and Birthing

If comparisons between authoring and birthing seem farfetched, we should recall, first, that "to author" originally meant "to make to grow, originate, promote, increase." While the root suggests insemination, it is useful to notice the connection between writing and procreation. Hawthorne himself called attention to this analogy, most notably in "The Artist of the Beautiful," surely his most important meditation on his role as artist prior to the major novels. In that story the narrator contrasts the "offspring" of the idealistic artist Owen Warland (who is, true to his name, his "own war land"), and that of the carnal couple, Robert and Annie Danforth. In what seems like an authorial regression to his pre-married life, Hawthorne stages a dramatic conflict between these "children," for Owen's "spiritualized" butterfly, the product of an almost autistic artistic sensibility, is crushed by the "natural" child of the married couple: "With a wavering movement, and emitting a tremulous radiance, the butterfly struggled, as it were, towards the infant, and was about to alight upon his finger. But, while it still hovered in the air, the little Child of Strength . . . made a snatch at the marvellous insect, and compressed it in his hand. . . . The blacksmith, by main force, unclosed the infant's hand, and found within the palm a small heap of glittering fragments, whence the Mystery of Beauty had fled for ever." It is apparent, then, that in this 1844 story Hawthorne could not imagine a meeting point between the natural and the ideal, the biological and the cultural forms of creation. By contrast, the adulteress represents a fusion of these creative processes. In an obvious sense she incorporates the dichotomies of "The Artist of the Beautiful," for in her giving birth to Pearl she emulates (if illicitly) the creativity of Robert and Annie, while in projecting her social reforms for women she models the idealistic thoughtwork of Owen. However, at a kind of juncture or meeting point between the biological and the cultural, Hester produces her astonishing art: "She had in her nature a rich, voluptuous, Oriental characteristic,—a taste for the gorgeously beautiful, which, save in the exquisite productions of her needle, found nothing else, in all the possibilities of her life, to exercise itself upon." The passage carefully balances "voluptuous" against "exquisite," the passional against the refined, suggesting a more complex understanding of authorial creativity than Hawthorne demonstrated in "The Artist of the Beautiful." Not only did Hawthorne reveal a similar "voluptuousness" in his love letters, but upon the birth of Una he expressed a similar sense of "falling" into the biological, material world, a fortunate fall into the realm of care, human relations, and pain. . . .

Guilt of Hawthorne and Hester

It is as if Hawthorne were announcing his transformation from an Owen Warland into a Hester Prynne, a conversion from the inhabitant of a "cloud-region" to a participant in "the sombre texture of humanity." For writer and protagonist both, the child is mother to the authentic artist.

To this point I have emphasized what might be termed the "empowering" or "liberating" qualities of Hawthorne's identification with the adulteress. At the very least, Hawthorne sets aside a trivializing self-image as artist in favor of a "devilish" author who "gushes forth" his words. As part of that transformation, Hawthorne identifies with females in general and female writers in particular in their struggle with marginality and silence. At the same time, Hawthorne seems to affirm the carnal origins of his own creativity, ironically dismissing the "shrunken" male artist such as Owen (and one might speculate, Dimmesdale as well). Yet, as Frederick Crews has forcefully observed, "even for the most bounteously passionate of Hawthorne's characters . . . art and guilt are intertwined." The novel registers this sense of guilt, for despite Hester's obvious appeal—her heroism, her endurance, her daring—she remains a censured figure, not only by surrounding characters, but by the narrator himself. . . .

More importantly for purposes of this analysis, Hawthorne's often critical characterization of Hester leads us to consider additional meanings of "adulterate." What about the process of "adulteration" might cause Hawthorne to feel guilt or shame? Or, pursuing another possibility, might Hawthorne *need* to adulterate in order to succeed as an artist, especially in his treatment of the adulterous heroine? In its widest application, "to adulterate" means "to render spurious or counterfeit; to falsify, corrupt, debase, especially by the admixture of baser ingredients." Hawthorne lived in a kind of global terror of "adulteration," a dread that he practiced such "counterfeiting" every time he took up the pen. . . .

Though Hester seems to provide a new conception of the romantic artist, at the same time Hawthorne continues to wrestle with these latent demons of artistic guilt. It is at least suggestive that as Hester confronts the community upon the scaffold, the narrator directs the reader's vision to "the unadulterated sunshine," an apt figure for divine judgment, "the light of common day," and perhaps even a Platonic realm beyond this fallen world. Hester's adultery transgresses all three worlds, for she has sinned against her religion, evicted herself from the "common" world, and "fallen" into "the sombre texture of humanity" out of the "cloud-regions". . . .

Hester as Self-Censorship

I suggest, then, that the novel censures Hester in part because her "sin" of "adultery" implicitly recalls for the writer his own sins of authorial "adulteration." But in another sense, a far more cynical and yet self-protecting sense, the author *uses* adulteration to his advantage, and his female protagonist practices this same cunning art. In addition to the general definition discussed earlier, "adulterate" has traditionally referred to a process of preparing a product for sale by "mixing in baser elements." Unquestionably Hawthorne sensed that he could achieve an authorial "ten strike" by "mixing in the baser elements" of sex, adultery, and ministerial misdeeds. . . .

To survive in the marketplace, the author/adulteress *must* compromise, must balance internal vision against external form, subversive drives against communally sanctioned genres. Ironically it is as an adulteress that Hawthorne found the resolution of that conflict between "public man" and "artist," between the financially solvent and imaginatively inspired personae. Once he had entered the marketplace as a scandal, he could exploit the "shame" for financial benefit, an attitude made transparent by his composing "The Custom-House." Indeed, Hawthorne frequently mentioned that it was the satiric sketch which drew the most attention to his text. . . .

Thus Hawthorne the artist was indeed a kind of adulteress, for he transgressed vocational and gender boundaries, acknowledged sexuality as a prime mover in art and culture, confessed to "adulterating" the truth in all its possible manifestations, and made due with an independent source of income closely linked to his "adulterous" behavior.

A Woman's Calling

Carolyn R. Maibor

Carolyn R. Maibor is assistant professor of English at Framingham State College. She has taught at the University of Montreal, Simmons College (Boston), and Brandeis University and has published articles on Ralph Waldo Emerson.

Prominent in the nineteenth-century struggle for women's rights was the issue of women's work and social reform. In the 1830s and 1840s, women who chose to work for public reforms such as temperance, abolition, and women's rights were scorned and discouraged, especially if their work involved public speaking; they were often forced to persuade men to speak for them. The degree of Hester's feminism rests on why, at the end, she leaves her beloved daughter and an easy way of life to return to Boston. Here she puts into action the radical speculation about the condition and future of women. She contributes charitable action and quiet advice to the society of women but avoids the public preaching of Anne Hutchinson. Some critics have claimed that Hester returns as a means of atonement, but Carolyn R. Maibor argues that she returns to embrace her vocation as a counselor and reformer. The novel's narrator qualifies the feminism of the book by informing us that women's lot will change "in Heaven's own time." But Hester fulfills her role as a prophetess, hastening the arrival of the time when society will change to benefit women.

In looking at *The Scarlet Letter* through the lens of work, and focusing particularly on the character of Hester, I think the novel can be seen as a working out of many of Hawthorne's own frustrations and ambivalence about vocational choices and the limits of those choices (particularly for women), as well as the need to find a balance between satisfying the inner, "unquiet impulse," and the practical demands of life. The need to make a contribution to society, as Hawthorne suggests at the very beginning in "The Custom-House" essay, is also a powerful force in the novel, and provides an alternative way of thinking about the controversial ending.

Near the beginning of his novel, once Hester's prison term has ended, Hawthorne attempts to explain to his readers why she does not leave the community at once for some place where she could hide her identity, since, as he acknowledges, her sentence did not require her to stay, and he offers three different possibilities. The "secret" reason, which Hester hides from herself, is her belief in the union, although "unrecognized on earth," between herself and her lover. The second reason, the one she "compelled herself to believe," was the hope that the martyrdom of the daily shame she would endure in New England would eventually purify her soul. The interpretation that Hawthorne himself gives of her decision to remain is less ethereal:

> But there is a fatality, a feeling so irresistible and inevitable that it has the force of doom, which almost invariably compels human beings to linger around and haunt, ghost-like, the spot where some great and marked event has given the color to their lifetime; and still the more irresistibly, the darker the tinge that saddens it. Her sin, her ignominy, were the roots which she had struck into the soil. . . .

Whatever the reasons, Hester had "struck her roots" into the soil of New England, and is left to find a way to support herself and her daughter in a town in which she cannot conceal her identity.

The Seamstress

While her situation is lonely, Hawthorne quickly tells us that at least she "incurred no risk of want. She possessed an art that sufficed, even in a land that afforded comparatively little scope for its exercise, to supply food for her thriving infant and herself." That art, as Hawthorne refers to it, "almost the only one within a woman's grasp," is, of course, that of needlework. We know from the first time we see Hester on the scaffold, and witness along with the crowd the "gorgeous luxuriance" of the letter she has embroidered, that Hester is a remarkably skilled seamstress. Although the Puritans are not known for having much need for such handiwork, there are enough formal occasions, Hawthorne tells us, for elaborate, ceremonial costumes, and Hester's work quickly becomes "the fashion," so much so that "she had ready and fairly requited employment for as many hours as she saw fit to occupy with her needle." But while Hester's work provides for her practical needs, and seems to fill "a gap which must otherwise have remained vacant," giving her "a part to perform in the world," Hester's sewing is not the moral equivalent of Hawthorne's writing, though several readers of the novel have made that connection. Hester, Hawthorne makes clear, does not sew for pleasure (although he admits it might give her some release as a means of self-expression) or to quiet an unsatisfied internal impulse: Hester sews for money—and just enough for a plain and ascetic subsistence. She does sew elaborate outfits for Pearl, but Hawthorne relates this to part of her self-imposed penance, so like the scarlet letter are Pearl's dresses. Rather than being called to her needlework, in the Emersonian sense of a vocation, Hester uses it as a substitute: "She had in her nature a rich, voluptuous, Oriental characteristic,—a taste for the gorgeously beautiful, which, save in the exquisite productions of her needle, found nothing else, in all the possibilities of her life, to exercise itself upon"—suggesting that the more elaborate her sewing, the more of a profound lack she was feeling in the rest of her life. Furthermore, although she serves the community by fulfilling its vain need for highly decorative ceremonial attire, this is not the kind of self-fulfilling sharing in "the united effort of mankind" that Hawthorne dreams about in "The Custom-House." Indeed, Hawthorne tells us that although her work forces her continued intercourse with society, "there was nothing that made her feel she belonged to it." And Hawthorne is always attuned to the dangers inherent in this isolation. . . .

Work in Society

Hester is not, of course, completely cut off from her community. She has her part to play in society, contributing the required festive attire as well as making clothes for the poor, and, Hawthorne tells us, "she was quick to acknowledge her sisterhood with the race of man, whenever benefits were to be conferred." These benefits, however, are only bestowed in "the darkened houses" of the sick and dying. Meeting her fellow townsfolk on the streets during the day, Hester would not raise her head to greet them or receive their greetings, about which Hawthorne cryptically notes, "This might be pride, but was so like humility, that it produced all the softening influence of the latter quality on the public mind." Her good works and her presumed humility cause society to show Hester, for the most part, "a more benign countenance than she cared to be favored with, or, perchance, than she deserved." Not only does Hawthorne encourage the reader to question the motivations for Hester's good works by doubting whether she deserves to be shown such kindness, but even more curiously, he adds that despite the contributions she makes to others, she does not want the community's kindness. What could be her motivation for performing such deeds if she does not want to be forgiven and accepted into the society? Moreover, what, in her performance of these works, undermines their merit? This work could be, like the reason Hester tries to convince herself of for remaining in New England, performed with the desire for "cleansing" herself, and therefore not the selfless act that would have earned her the "benign countenance" of the community. Hester's willingness to act as a "sister of mercy" might also be explained, as Nina Baym suggests, by her desire "to live unmolested, not because she believes in doing good." A third possibility is that this work provides her with a form of power she can exert over the community, and by her (and her letter's) constant presence, a form of punishment for the sentence they inflicted on her. . . .

Hester as Reformer

In addition to the several warnings included in the text about the dangers of Hester's solitude teaching her "much amiss," Hawthorne is also careful to show the benefits of Hester's estrangement from the establishment. Her separation from the community is a necessary component in her continued ability to think outside of the accepted boundaries which society had established, and is an essential aspect of her arriving at her ultimate purpose and means of serving both herself and society. Hester's seclusion frees her, we are told in [the chapter titled] "Another View of Hester," from measuring her "ideas of right and wrong by any standard external to herself. . . ." It allows her a "freedom of speculation," which although not uncommon, as Hawthorne tells us, on "the other side of the Atlantic," had her Puritan neighbors suspected her of it, they would have considered it "a deadlier crime than that stigmatized by the scarlet letter." Her estrangement from society allows her a unique vantage point from which to view, and criticize, human institutions. However, the speculation, in her "lonesome cottage," which leads her to question not her breaking of society's laws and codes, but the system which put those codes in place, brings her to a dangerous and desperate sense of hopelessness, and causes her to ask whether the life available to women was even worth living. And, Hawthorne tells us, she had already decided that the answer for herself was undoubtedly no: "A tendency to speculation, though it may keep woman quiet, as it does man, yet makes her sad." That sadness comes in part from the helplessness she feels in confronting what she sees as amiss in those institutions. . . .

Ultimately, however, Hester does come to see a value in staying and fighting for change, rather than totally withdrawing herself and her daughter from society. The change begins to occur, ironically, in her attempt to boost Dimmesdale's sense of self worth. In their meeting in the forest, seven years after Hester's condemnation, Dimmesdale confesses his feeling of despair, and his guilt at his hypocritical life. But Hester insists on the reality of the good deeds Dimmesdale performs in the community and thus on his deserving the reverence his parishioners show him: "Your present life is not less holy, in very truth, than it seems in people's eyes. Is there no reality in the penitence thus sealed and witnessed by good works?" Dimmesdale, however, admits that there has been no penitence, and the people's reverence, like the kindness Hawthorne discusses in their treatment of Hester passing on the street, is more than he cares to be favored with, and, indeed, more than he deserves. . . .

Hester, although misled in some of the lessons she takes from her solitary speculation and erring in some of her actions, has, finally, an appreciation of the "social" aspect of work—the contribution to other—as demonstrated in her remarks to Dimmesdale about his good works. Furthermore, as her words to Dimmesdale also indicate, she comes to place an emphasis on doing. When Dimmesdale turns to her after learning Chillingworth's true identity, wondering how he can continue to live any longer with such an enemy, yet unable to see any other options beyond lying down on the leaves and dying at once, Hester loses her patience with him, aware for once, perhaps, of the blindness caused by his self-involvement. . . .

Leadership and Vocation

Although Hester does say that this time [of mutual happiness for man and woman] will come "when the world should have grown ripe for it, in Heaven's own time," there is nothing to preclude the fact that Hester's "counseling center," as [Sacvan] Bercovitch calls it, might play an important part in helping the world "grow ripe," and there is nothing in Hawthorne's description that insists that the time is necessarily far off. As Hawthorne recounts, Hester had at one time believed that she herself might be the prophetess of this divine new truth, and although she comes to the decision that this mission will not be entrusted to a woman "stained with sin," she may well hold out the possibly that one of her "patients" might yet be that prophetess. . . .

And as thinking about that weighty responsibility in relation to her own daughter initially brings Hester to contemplate the situation facing the rest of womankind, it is not surprising then, that having brought Pearl to a satisfactory position in life (albeit with the help Chillingworth's money adds in giving Pearl some degree of freedom not readily available to all women), Hester would feel a calling to return to the site of her own most trying struggles to help develop "the germ and blossom" of other young women amid their various difficulties. The mission her spirit summons her to, which Hester originally encouraged Dimmesdale to seek out, the "real life" she finds in New England, comes in her role as counselor to women. . . .

While it is true that Hester does not, in fact, "overturn" the social system, it cannot be said that she does not change it. If we think, for example, of the Puritan women portrayed at the beginning of the story, the gossips who refer to Hester as the "brazen hussy," who think the leaders of town have not been harsh enough with her, and who avoid getting too close to her, physically, and compare them to the young women of the town at the end of the novel (presumably the daughters of these "gossips") who, of their own accord, seek out Hester's advice at her cottage, we can see that although Hester's "revolution" has begun from her own internal growth, that growth seems to inspire others in their own self-development. Her new position as counselor to women allows Hester a degree of influence in the community, exercised not through dictating "group action," but through a sharing of ideas. . . .

Hester chooses to return to New England (and the constraints that that implies) for the "real life" of meaningful work she has carved out for herself, in which she uses her personal growth to help others in theirs. She is able to work on the changes she views as necessary for building a more just and humane society, not by quitting society (by beginning anew, as Bercovitch writes), or by tearing it down, but by effecting a gradual change of institutions by helping to effect a personal change within its participants. The mature Hester at the end of the novel has moved away from the absolutism of "give me liberty" (through the complete dismantling of society) or "give me death" (by suicide) to the subtler recognition that change is gradual and that meaningful individual triumphs are only achieved in connection to others. Hester, in other words, has found what Hawthorne claims to be looking for in "The Custom-House": a way to serve mankind and still the "unquiet impulse" that haunted her previous life in New England.

Living Against Nature in Puritan New England

Frederick Newberry

Frederick Newberry, professor of English at Duquesne University in Pittsburgh, is a widely published scholar on Hawthorne and has for many years served as editor of the Nathaniel Hawthorne Review.

In the following viewpoint, Frederick Newberry asserts that Hawthorne shows his own ambiguity about the Old and New Worlds through his characterization of Hester and Pearl. The Puritans, among whom Hester lives, have fled the Old World culture partly on religious grounds. The Anglican Church of England bore far too much resemblance to the hated Catholic Church of Rome to suit Puritan dissenters. Especially obnoxious to the Puritans were the culture's lavish clothing and decorations and the Anglican Church's use of ornate religious art and icons. Yet upper-class Puritan leaders clung to rich adornments during festivals and holidays, while the lower classes were ordered by law to dress simply, in keeping with their stations. In the novel, according to Newberry, this stark plainness is emblematic of suppressed nature. Dressing herself in somber gray yet sewing sumptuous clothes for Pearl, Hester projects onto her daughter the true, full nature of womanhood.

Although Hawthorne's indignation over being dismissed from his post is embedded in "The Custom-House," a crucial element of that indignation finds expression in a historical perspective that both includes and transcends Hawthorne's personal case. A Jonathan Pue, a Chaucer, or a Burns could rely on the traditional support of his government

Frederick Newberry, *Hawthorne's Divided Loyalties*. Cranbury, NJ: Fairleigh Dickinson University Press, 1987.

and culture. England had a history of valuing its artists, while America did not. The recognition was not new to Hawthorne, but he experienced it now more fully and personally than earlier; and in so doing he discovered the subject necessary for the novel that had so long eluded him: the very origins of anti-aesthetic, anti-imaginative prejudice of New England. Lying at the heart of *The Scarlet Letter*, therefore, exists a fairly large measure of hostility aimed at Puritan America's conventional mistrust of art. More fully articulated than in previous works, such mistrust went hand in hand with the cultural separation between New and Old Worlds. And more fully evident than heretofore appears a division in Hawthorne's loyalties to these separate worlds because of his determination to recover an English aesthetic for himself and America. Bitterness over the circumstances of his removal from the Custom House may have been the immediate cause of his deciding to undertake a full-scale recovery, and yet the substance of many of the historical tales virtually imply as much, while "The Old Manse" surely predicts the method.

Nature and Cultural Conflict

Nevertheless, more cogently than in Hawthorne's previous work, *The Scarlet Letter* is about the cultural history of Puritan America, and the conflict between dominant and recessive qualities of Puritanism more or less defined by 1649. As Hawthorne sees it, the seven-year period covered by the novel's action is pivotal, not only in New England history but also, and most relevantly, in English history. With his knowledge of colonial American history, in conjunction with his considerable knowledge of English history, Hawthorne again traces the growth of the dominating forces of Puritanism: severity, rigidity, intolerance, iconoclasm, militancy, and persecution. But he also explores to a far greater extent than earlier the attractive but recessive qualities of early Puritans that form a part of their English heritage: sympathy, charity, gaiety, communal celebration, respect for tradition, and appreciation of art. These qualities—personified especially by Dimmesdale, Hester, and Pearl—are posed as alternatives to the dominant traits of the Puritan majority. Linked with English antiquity, these alternatives, if they had flourished in the New World, would have given an entirely different tone and direction to New England and thus to American history as a whole. . . .

As Endicott comes to power, Dimmesdale dies and Hester and Pearl remove themselves from the New World. Pearl is altogether lost to America, while Hester returns appreciably altered in character. Through these figures, preeminently, *The Scarlet Letter* dramatizes mitigating alternatives to Puritanic militancy, persecution, and iconoclasm. It is clearly no accident that these appealing figures are lost to the colony, for the same pattern of survival and loss extends to minor figures, including the gentlest of the women watching Hester's disgrace at the novel's opening: unlike the blood-thirsty "gossips," she is dead in the final scene seven years later. . . .

The Scarlet Letter places Renaissance color and love of exotic beauty, embodied by Hester and Pearl, in striking relief against the stark, joyless modes and manners of the Puritan majority. . . .

A Woman's Memory

Hester's memory of her girlhood in "our old home" is no less fond or significant than Tobias and Dorothy Pearson's memory of England in [Hawthorne's story] "The Gentle Boy." Nevertheless, her English past and the optimism suggested in her duplication of the Pilgrim moves to Holland and America vividly contrast with "the rude market-place of the Puritan settlement" where, upon the scaffold, she stands holding Pearl, her public sin and perhaps her private shame exposed. Hester has been influenced with a sufficient amount of Calvinistic doctrine to feel that "the scaffold of the pillory was a point of view that revealed . . . the entire track along which she had been treading, since her happy infancy." So much for sloughing the skin of Old World corruption in coming to the New World. But while Hester acknowledges her predetermined reenactment of original sin, she evidently has not observed the orthodox logic of how she ought to behave as a result of it. She has clearly spent her months in prison in rather unrepentant and even heretical fashion. As Hester stands exposed before her neighbors in all the beauty of her person, dress, and scarlet letter, she reveals something quite different from evidentiary Puritan atonement, something far more in keeping with her Old World reflections.

In view of Puritan sumptuary laws prohibiting the general populace from wearing lavish dress, and from the vantage of Puritan opposition to religious images, Hawthorne describes Hester's appearance and the effects of her needlework in terms anomalous to the historical setting. He continues to associate her with the Old World and, more specifically, with its aristocratic (even ecclesiastical) art, presumably inimical to Puritanism. Hester, we later learn, has "fingers that could have embroidered a monarch's robe." Through the artful stitching witnessed in the scarlet letter, she produces a "specimen of her delicate and imaginative skill of which the dames of a court might gladly have availed themselves, to add the richer and more spiritual adornment of human ingenuity to their fabrics of silk and gold."

The beautiful artifact initially repels the colonists, who later persecute Hester and ostracize her from the community not only because she has sinned but also because she has created a distinctly non-Puritan form of beauty from the symbol of her sin. Given the Calvinistic side of her ruminations, Hester should have expected nothing less, and so it would seem that she contributes to her own alienation. She has fashioned "wild" and "picturesque" clothing, and she has also embroidered the scarlet letter with an artistic "luxuriance of fancy." Together, these products of her skill and imagination have "a splendor in accordance with the taste of the age, but greatly beyond what was allowed by the sumptuary regulations of the colony." Some of the spectators obviously make no mistake in thinking that Hester "make[s] a pride out what" the magistrates "meant for a punishment."

From a Puritan point of view of providential signs, Hester's confinement in the dark jail should have allowed enough time for her beauty to fade and for guilt to shadow forth its physical effects. But her appearance belies these unsanctified effects anticipated by those Puritans "who had before known her, and had expected to behold her dimmed and obscured by a disastrous cloud." Instead, they are "astonished, and even startled, to perceive how her beauty shone out, and made a halo of misfortune and ignominy in which she was enveloped." Preconceptions give way to uncomfortable perceptions; and the Puritans have every reason to be alarmed over what they see. As if illuminated by the traditional aureole in Christian art and "transfigured" by the scarlet letter, Hester appears before the crowd as if in resemblance of a once-revered icon, but now an idolatrous image of the Virgin Mary. The historical moment of transition from Old to New World is the crucial context. Like John Wilson, the assembled Puritans have been "nurtured at the rich bosom of the English Church." They are accordingly familiar with the Roman Catholic imagery in the churches having survived destruction under Edward VI and in those having been readorned under James I and Charles I. What they sense in Hester's image is partly what they abhor in the Church of England: the religious art that to their minds constitutes not only idolatrous images but threatening signs of a renewed affiliation with Rome on the part of the Stuarts.

Beautiful, illuminated, and "transfigured"—her sin notwithstanding—Hester appears before the Puritans as if mocking their severe religious and aesthetic sensibilities. But at the same time, because of her sin, she poses as a shameful contrast to the traditional image her appearance suggests.

Two Puritan colonists on their way to church, dressed plainly in black and white. This stark plainness of their clothing becomes emblematic of their suppressed nature. Three Lions/ Hulton Archive/Getty Images.

Had there been a Papist among the crowd of Puritans, he might have seen in this beautiful woman, so picturesque in

> her attire and mien, and with the infant at her bosom, an object to remind him of the image of Divine Maternity, which so many illustrious painters have vied with one another to represent; something which should remind him, indeed, but only by contrast, of that sacred image of sinless motherhood, whose infant was to redeem the world. Here, there was the taint of deepest sin in the most sacred quality of human life, working such effect, that the world was only the darker for this woman's beauty, and the more lost for the infant that she had borne.

Old World Catholicism and Hester

The introduction of a Roman Catholic point of view, no more anomalous than historically resonant, temporarily completes the aesthetic resemblance Hester and Pearl bear to the Virgin Mary and Christ. Hawthorne then safely denies the suitability of the resemblance by accentuating Hester's sin. Still, we are left with uncomfortable dualisms of purity and sin, redemption and damnation, which, as it turns out, interlock in a paradoxical image symbolizing the spiritual and historical complexities at issue throughout the novel.

The Anglo-Catholic imagery associated with Hester and her art does not entirely disappear following the evocation of Madonna and Child. She exchanges her beautiful clothes for a gray robe and she hides her beautiful hair beneath a cap. Pious Bostonians, who believe in the efficacious logic of "visible sanctity," observe her "penance" and "good deeds" for seven years; and thus, by some trick of perception, memory, or Federal Theology, they come to believe that the scarlet letter has meanings other than its original designation for adultery. Even those who cannot forget the "black scandal" see with no apparent ill reflection on their divine covenant and errand that the scarlet letter "had the effect of the cross on a nun's bosom," or that it "imparted to the wearer a kind of sacredness." Altered in luxurious beauty though it is, Hester's presence somehow manages to sustain an impression "majestic and statue-like." And so from Madonna, to nun with a cross, to statue, Hester's metamorphosis retains a resemblance to icons, wholly anathema to the Puritan setting. Nothing inconsistent finally obtains in the fact that when Hester supports the fallen Dimmesdale in the last scaffold scene she once again evokes the Madonna; for their pose pictorially suggests the traditional pietà in Christian art, the whole scene having unmistakable overtones of a crucifixion.

Puritan Use of Hester

... Conforming to his view that the first-generation Puritans were closer to Renaissance sensibility than were their descendants, Hawthorne also shows how Boston's upper classes actually come to patronize Hester's art. While the community has left behind some of the strict divisions in the social and ecclesiastical hierarchy of English culture, it has instituted its own forms of rank and status—social, civil, and clerical—still bearing resemblance to those in the mother country. Just as Hester's art is worthy of cultivated tastes of the monarch and nobility in England, so it is in demand by the higher orders of Puritan society....

Eventually Hester's needlework becomes the "fashion" among the upper ranks of Puritan society, a chief reason being that her art "really filled a gap which must otherwise have remained vacant" in the community.

The appeal of Hester's art to this first generation of Puritans that once lived in England would be less surprising were Hester's art not associated with the sin out of which the luxurious needlework first emerges for public view, and were it not, moreover, reminiscent of royal and even perhaps "papist" aesthetic forms. Hawthorne's ironic explanation for this rather egregious lapse in Puritan scruple is that "Vanity, it may be, chose to mortify itself, by putting on, for ceremonies of pomp and state, the garments that had been wrought by her sinful hands." The extent of this mortification is adequately revealed in the novel's opening scene and more fully yet in the election day scene near its conclusion.

In his treatment of Pearl, Hawthorne depicts other Old World survivals in early America. When, after the novel's opening scene, Hester exchanges her dress for the gray robe, she gives her striking mode of apparel on the scaffold to Pearl. The child's dresses, made of the "richest tissues," display the aesthetic range of Hester's "imaginative faculty." Transferring the splendor of her clothes to Pearl, Hester also transfers the halo of her beauty: "So magnificent was the small figure, . . . and such was the splendor of Pearl's own proper beauty, shining through the gorgeous robes . . . that there was an absolute circle of radiance around her." . . .

Pearl and the Puritans

Embodying the very art of her mother, which is engrained in traditions antithetical to Puritanism, Pearl attacks the Puritan children like "some half-fledged angel of judgement,—whose mission was to punish the sins of the rising generation." In her beauty, imaginative play, harmony with nature, and ties with ancient traditions—all the valorized qualities carefully assembled in "The Old Manse" and "The Custom-House"—Pearl represents the best values out of which American culture might be built, the very elements missing in second-generation Puritans (and missing to a great degree in the first). Even in its childhood games, the second generation forecasts Puritanic obsessions in the latter half of the seventeenth century: "scourging Quakers; or taking scalps in a sham-fight with the Indians; or scaring one another with freaks of imitative witchcraft." That the children also play at going to church indicates with what piety they will later persecute the Quakers in the 1650s, massacre the Indians in King Philip's War, and convict their brethren of witchcraft in the early 1690s. . . .

Art and Nature Leave Boston

When Hester and Pearl leave New England a year after Dimmesdale's final scene on the scaffold, they take with them the aesthetic continuity between England and America that they have represented. They leave America, in other words, aesthetically barren—with the very "gap" that Hester once filled and that Pearl could one day fill in her turn. Their departure, coincident with the rise of the second generation of Puritans, suggests the magnitude of the historical schism evaluated by Hawthorne in *The Scarlet Letter*. England and Europe, not America, are cast not only as the cultural sources but also the ultimate repositories of art. Accordingly, after Hester returns to Boston some years later, she does not resume her needlework except in one instance: to embroider "a baby-garment, with such a lavish richness of golden fancy as would have raised a public tumult, had any infant, thus apparelled, been shown to our sombre-hued community." Because their origins lay in England, most first-generation Puritans could accept this form of dress in Pearl and even want to possess other articles for itself evincing Hester's art. But the second generation, led by Endicott, becomes Puritanic. Unlike its counterparts in England who experience the Restoration, it retains the iconoclastic legacy of Civil War extremists. Thus, at the novel's close, Hester must send the only expression of her art back to Europe—to Pearl and her child, symbols of a cultural transmission and of a potential artistic heritage not yet acceptable in America. The ultimate logic of Puritan severity and inconoclasm leads to restrictions altogether abortive to the development of an aesthetic tradition in the New World upon which Hawthorne and other native American artists might draw. Because he inherited an aesthetic void from New England's past, while nevertheless imagining a historical situation in which Hester could defy her persecutors and create an art constituting the basis for a tradition, it became Hawthorne's task to resurrect the tradition in his own day. His too, no less than Hester's, was a magnificent act of defiance, an assertion not only of art's legitimate place in America but also of its freedom to borrow and adapt cross-cultural traditions for reasons transcending the provincial biases of any time and place.

Woman as Outsider

Kristin Herzog

Kristin Herzog, an independent scholar based in Durham, North Carolina, is the author of Finding Their Voice: Peruvian Women's Testimonies of War *(1993).*

According to Kristin Herzog, the extent of Hester's refusal to accept the Puritan view of women is figured by her identification with New England's Native Americans. Like them, she lives on the margins of society, and her ideas, especially about women, are so wild and free that, had her views been known, she would have been considered as dangerous as an Indian. Even so, she is seen as more of an outlaw in the marketplace than the Native Americans and pirates who freely mingle in the crowd. Hester's radicalism and strength, which are the result of her nature and her life on the edges, frightens Dimmesdale. She (the woman) makes arrangements to run away with him on a pirate ship, while he (the male) is too inept and weak to even help in the plan. Hester is shown to be capable of disregarding civilized boundaries with ease.

> It might be that a sluggish bond-servant, or an undutiful child . . . was to be corrected at the whipping post. It might be, that an Antinomian, a Quaker, or other heterodox religionist was to be scourged out of the town, or an idle and vagrant Indian, whom the white man's fire-water had made riotous about the streets, was to be driven with stripes into the shadow of the forest. It might be, too, that a witch, like old Mistress Hibbins, the bitter-tempered widow of the magistrate, was to die upon the gallows.

The Scarlet Letter is a story set at the rough edge of civilization. The dark forest is still ominously near, and the dark dangers from foreign servants, untamed children, stubborn heretics, idle Indians, or hell-bound witches seem to threaten the progress of Puritan civilization's sacred new orders. The passage quoted above foreshadows in a variety of images Hester Prynne's emergence from the prison: while she is not a bond-servant, she is bound by the bonds of marriage to an unloved, old husband who sent her alone to a foreign continent. She also binds herself in love to a man whose name she will not utter. She is certainly no child, but the gruff English-born matrons who gossip about her fate and her character call her "brazen hussy" and "naughty baggage," and the image of the "undutiful child" prepares us for getting to know [Hester's daughter] Pearl. Her lonely exile at the border of the town will later make her an Antinomian in thought, and the author has already reminded us of another freethinker, "sainted Ann Hutchinson," with whom Hester is symbolically identified through the wild rosebush at the prison door. Hester herself might have become the foundress of a religious sect or a prophetess if she had not borne a child and had lived a purer life. She certainly is as much an outcast as any Quaker in the Puritan colony, and she bears public abuse with a Quaker's dignity. Her freedom of speculation makes her as dangerous as any "heterodox religionist" who was "then common enough on the other side of the Atlantic."

Woman and Outcasts

The image of the Indian appears at the beginning and at the end of the novel, and throughout the story a certain wildness and passion in Hester's character is, directly or indirectly, identified with the American Indian. This "aboriginal" aspect of Hester's femininity is not the only trait, however, which separates her from the Puritan women around her. She is also an alien with a touch of the exotic, in spite of her apparently uneventful childhood in rural England. "She had in her nature a rich, voluptuous, Oriental characteristic,—a taste for the gorgeously beautiful." In her "otherness," she is a woman of awesome power.

Hester's Indian or "aboriginal" characteristics have been strengthened by social isolation which caused her to wander "without rule or guidance, in a moral wilderness; as vast, as intricate and shadowy, as the untamed forest." Arthur Dimmesdale, after the climactic union in the forest, is filled not only with hope and joy, but "with fear betwixt them, and a kind of horror at her boldness." In part Hester's attitude grew out of her "native courage and activity," but it was also a consequence of her outlaw existence. "Her intellect and heart had their home, as it were, in desert places, where she roamed as freely as the wild Indian in his woods." At the beginning of the novel, she is described as "impulsive and passionate" and yet showing a "natural dignity and force of character." The "desperate recklessness of her mood" is hidden behind a "serene deportment." This description parallels a portrayal of the Indians toward the end of the story, when they have flocked to town at the New England holiday.

> A party of Indians—in their savage finery of curiously embroidered deer-skirt robes, wampum belts, red and yellow ochre, and feathers, and armed with the bow and arrow and stone-headed spear—stood apart, with countenances of inflexible gravity, beyond what even a Puritan aspect could attain. Nor, wild as were these painted barbarians, were they the wildest feature of the scene. This distinction could more justly be claimed by some mariners....

Hester as Outlaw and Divine Mother

Hester's inner spiritual and emotional struggle shows the same polarity [as her outward appearance]. On the one hand, she is a typical romantic heroine who can say after a meeting with her husband, "Be it sin or no ... I hate the man." She

A group of townsfolk making an arrest of a woman accused of witchcraft in Salem, Massachusetts. Women accused of witchcraft often lived on the margins of society, like Hester Prynne. Mansell/Time & Life Pictures/Getty Images.

can remind Dimmesdale that what they did had "a consecration of its own." When she broods about the dilemma of womanhood, she wanders "without a clew in the dark labyrinth of her mind." At times, a fearful doubt strives to possess her soul "whether it were not better to send Pearl at once to heaven, and go herself to such futurity as Eternal Justice should provide." When she finds new hope after the reunion with Dimmesdale in the forest, she is ready to flee with him on a ship that significantly is an outlaw vessel with a crew of "rough looking desperadoes" who are guilty of "depredations on the Spanish commerce." Hester is at times a "Fausta," boldly or desperately overstepping all boundaries of faith and tradition.

But there is a self-restraining side to Hester also. She upbraids herself for hating Chillingworth, though she cannot overcome her hate; she patiently bears insults, even from the poor whom she is helping; she is "a martyr indeed," although she does not pray for her enemies "lest, in spite of her forgiving aspirations, the words of the blessing should stubbornly twist themselves into a curse." Before as well as after Dimmesdale's death, she is free to go back to England but remains to do of her own free will what society had forced her to do. She becomes a [Virgin] Mary figure to whom people bring "all their sorrows and perplexities."

Thus Hester is not just a fallen Eve; she is a divine mother, a Sister of Mercy, a nun, a saint, an angel, a potential prophetess or foundress of a religious sect, and a martyr. Hester is an "able woman," a woman of strength "almost majestic in ... despair." She is a queenly figure who may have gotten her name from the biblical Esther. Queen Esther is a woman of courage, beauty, dignity, and selflessness. Hester Prynne has all these qualities. In contrast to many pliable, submissive women figures in the fiction of the 1850s, Hester has "combative energy," a "desperate recklessness of ... mood," "freedom of speculation," and "a mind of native courage and activity." She explores realms unimagined by Dimmesdale and by her society. . . .

Strength from Savaging

As a member of a Puritan colony and in love with a Puritan minister, she fights the demonic forces of the forest in herself when she tries hard not to hate or curse, not to take her own life or that of her child, not to join in with Mistress Hibbins's insane forest rites, and to keep love and mercy alive in her. Her Indian-ness, however, is also her strength. Her return to her old abode and her taking up the scarlet letter again of her own free will are the best expression of the two forces in her: an aboriginal freedom and an awesome power of commitment....

Hawthorne, especially in his tales, describes the early Puritan view of the Indian, but as a romantic writer he cherishes the vitality of the primitive life-force expressed in the American Indian. Therefore, on the one hand, Chillingworth's worst traits, according to Puritan rumors, were intensified by his contact with the Indians' Black Art, and Hester wanders in a "moral wilderness" like the Indian who roams in desert places; on the other hand, Hester's Indian-like qualities of strength, passion, endurance, dignity, and independence are deemed admirable and are contrasted with the narrow-mindedness of the Puritan system and the weakness of Dimmesdale. The Indian of the nineteenth century was alternately the symbol of humanity's childhood and Golden Age innocence and the lustful, cruel violator of American pastoral peace. But to Hawthorne, the Puritans are the more cruel violators. Throughout the Hawthorne canon, the Puritans' martial prowess against the Indian is exposed as inhuman.

Hester, then, is an example of a new American Eve. Her similarity to primitive Indians is not, as it would be in popular sentimental novels, a similarity in terms of childlike behavior, docility, and self-effacing nobility. It is instead a kinship on grounds of an unquenchable thirst for freedom, a vital power of imagination, as expressed in her needlework art, and a strength in endurance which looks merely stoic on the outside but allows her to turn the prejudices of society, the images of the "old" Eve, into symbols of victory. Hester does not use her inner freedom in an individualistic fashion; she builds community instead of destroying it, as her final way of life indicates. No American writer before Hawthorne had described a woman as powerful as Hester Prynne.

Leadership and Delicacy

Joyce W. Warren

Joyce W. Warren, professor of English at Queens College, City University of New York, directs the women's studies program at the college. She is the author of Fanny Fern: An Independent Woman *(1992) and* Women, Money, and the Law *(2005) as well as the editor of* The (Other) American Traditions: Nineteenth-Century Women Writers *(1993).*

In the following viewpoint, Joyce W. Warren argues that Hester and the other female protagonists in Hawthorne's four major novels defy nineteenth-century stereotypes of women—up to a degree. Hester, for example, is stronger than the male characters in The Scarlet Letter, *yet she never assumes a role of public leadership. This self-contradictory portrait of Hester derives from Hawthorne's sympathy with the plight of women, coupled with his distaste for all reformers, especially women reformers in the public arena. Hester is sympathetic in that she lacks the public reformer's egotism or love of attention; she accomplishes her goal as a sister of charity with strength but out of the public eye. According to Warren, Hawthorne was able to draw such a sympathetic (but not heroic) feminine and feminist character largely because of his observations of his wife, Sophia.*

The reader of Nathaniel Hawthorne's fiction cannot help but be struck by the vividness of the portrayals of certain of his female characters. To be sure, Hawthorne's fiction contains its share of conventional heroines, but in three of his novels Hawthorne was able to go beyond this stereotyped image of American femininity to produce real flesh-and-blood women. Hester Prynne, Zenobia, Miriam—all are center-of-

Joyce W. Warren, *The American Narcissus: Individualism and Women in Nineteenth-Century American Fiction*. Piscataway, NJ: Rutgers University Press, 1984.

stage characters who cannot be downstaged by assertive male super-persons. It is true that Hawthorne's strong women are never allowed to pursue what might seem to be the implications of their characters; they do not become heroic leaders or independent public figures. Although this hesitation is owing in part to Hawthorne's belief in a conventional image of feminine behavior, it is also important to remember that there are no male heroes in Hawthorne's fiction either. Hawthorne did not countenance individual self-assertion in anyone—man or woman. . . .

A Conflicted View of Women

Hawthorne apparently believed that it was possible for women to possess talent and even genius, but he was concerned that the public exercise of talent would destroy what he regarded as the essence of a woman's femininity. In an 1830 essay on Anne Hutchinson, Hawthorne admonished: "Woman, when she feels the impulse of genius like a command of Heaven within her, should beware that she is relinquishing a part of the loveliness of her sex and obey the inward voice with sorrowing reluctance." Twenty-six years later Hawthorne still felt the same way. In a letter to [his wife] Sophia in 1856 he wrote that he was glad that she was not a public woman.

> With a brighter and deeper intellect than any other woman, thou hast never . . . prostituted thy self to the public. . . . It does seem to me to deprive women of all delicacy, it has pretty much such an effect on them as it would to walk abroad through streets, physically naked. . . .

A Complex View of Hester

It was Hawthorne's concern for feminine delicacy that complicated his position on women's rights. Though sensitive to and in sympathy with the plight of women in nineteenth-century society, he did not like reformers of any kind. He was also troubled by the fear that the independent woman would lose her femininity, that "ethereal essence, wherein she has her truest life." Yet his fiction is filled with references that reveal a sympathetic understanding of the problems that women faced. Hester's reflections in *The Scarlet Letter* (1850) on the injustices of woman's position—though they take her farther than Hawthorne is willing to follow—are not unsympathetically written. That Hawthorne agrees with Hester on the need for a more equitable treatment of women is apparent in his portrayal of the situation of Hester herself. He obviously believes that Hester was cruelly wronged by Chillingworth and comments on the injustice of the deformed old man's having persuaded a young girl into a loveless marriage at a time when "her heart knew no better." In Hester Prynne, Hawthorne created a woman of strength, intelligence, and resourcefulness, whose very existence gives the lie to those who would argue the natural inferiority of women. Hawthorne respects and admires Hester and the strength that enables her to withstand the scorn of the community and the failure of her lover.

Hester is a more admirable character than either of the men in the novel, both of whom are totally self-oriented. Of the three, only Hester is able to rise above the circumstances in which she finds herself. Chillingworth becomes a malicious fiend and Dimmesdale, a weak hypocrite. If Hawthorne draws back at the suggestion of restructuring society, if he fears the loss of feminine delicacy, he nevertheless sympathizes with the situation that would put a woman such as Hester Prynne at the mercy of arbitrary laws and masculine injustice. Though Hawthorne does not believe that Hester should attempt to change society, he sympathizes with her belief that one day, "in Heaven's own time, a new truth would be revealed, in order to establish the whole relationship between man and woman on a surer ground of mutual happiness."

If Hawthorne does not make Hester into a prophet and the leader of a sexual-social revolution, it is because, although he himself is very much aware of the problems that she perceives, he does not believe that she can accomplish any changes. Hawthorne was not a reformer, and he could not conceive of good coming through the imposition of abstract ideas. Those critics who see the ending of *The Scarlet Letter* as a cruel, misogynistic hamstringing of Hester's powers are reading into the novel a typically American concept of positive action. For Hawthorne, Hester's choice to remain with her child and then, after Pearl has grown up and gone her own way, to devote the remainder of her life to selflessly helping the people of her community as a kind of volunteer nurse and social worker is more indicative of strength of character than would be the solitary pursuit of an ideal, however worthy. . . .

Hawthorne disliked pretension and exaggerated self-importance. He was particularly impatient with people who concealed the truth about themselves by pretending to be what they were not. As he advised at the end of *The Scarlet Letter* and emphasized throughout his fiction: "Be true! Show freely to the world, if not your worst, yet some trait whereby the worst may be inferred!" . . .

Sophia's Influence on the Creation of Hester

Hawthorne's recognition of and respect for Sophia as an independent person and his simultaneous preference for gentle femininity in a wife help to explain why in his fiction he balanced his independent women characters with gentle dove-maidens. His ability to see women as separate beings enabled him to create women who were not abstractions. Hester, Zenobia, Miriam are not mere shadows of the male self. The strength and depth, the richness and passion that Hawthorne in his "inmost heart" knew could exist in a woman are magnificently developed in his strong women characters. But Hawthorne's conscious preference for maidenly virtues in a wife made it impossible for him to conceive of such a woman as a heroine because the traditional heroine was, after all, a potential wife. Although he admired and respected the independent woman, he did not encourage these qualities in his wife, particularly in her public role. Thus, two of his novels introduce an innocent young girl who is draped in white and, dovelike, maintains the gentle maidenly decorum of a virtuous heroine.

In *The Scarlet Letter* there is no such heroine because there is no danger that anyone will mistake Hester for a conventional heroine. Her story begins long after the marriage that usually ends the traditional heroine's story. She is a married woman, a mother, and an adultress before the action even starts. . . .

Hawthorne is best able to portray strong women characters when he does not place them at all in relation to a man. They are not the conventional marriage-candidate heroines who exist only to be found by men. Hester can be no one's fiancée, and there are hints that Zenobia and Miriam—always referred to as women, not as girls—have already been married or are in some way experienced. This status effectively disqualifies them for the role of traditional heroine. Since Hawthorne does not see such a woman in relation to a man, he can see her as an independent person, an individual. In fact, he himself sometimes identifies with these women—something he could never do with his dove-maidens, who are always the other. Hawthorne's emotional involvement in the story of Hester Prynne is suggested by the strong emotions he felt when he read the last scene of *The Scarlet Letter* to Sophia, just after writing it: "tried to read it, rather, for my voice swelled and heaved, as if I were tossed up and down in an ocean as it subsides after a storm." . . .

Hawthorne's view of life reflects a recognition of a duality that many of his contemporaries did not share. He saw good and evil, sunshine and shadow. And his attitude toward women is one aspect of this recognition of duality. . . .

Not a Transcendental Woman

It is apparent, then, that in his attitude toward women and in his portrayal of women in his fiction, Hawthorne differed markedly from his contemporaries among American writers. Why was Hawthorne able to conceive of women as persons when most nineteenth-century American male writers did not? In order to answer this question, it is necessary to recognize that Hawthorne also differed from his contemporaries in his attitude toward the dominant American culture. Hawthorne did not share his countrymen's enthusiastic belief in American individualism. Although a contemporary and sometime neighbor of [Transcendentalist thinker Ralph Waldo] Emerson's, Hawthorne dissented emphatically from the Transcendentalists' attitude toward the individual and the other. It is this difference in cultural attitudes, I believe, that explains Hawthorne's ability to portray women of substance in his fiction. . . .

Sympathizing with Hester

It is [the] ability to get "into the interior" of the other person that comes through in all of Hawthorne's fiction—a willingness to sympathize, a respect for each person as a fellow human being, and an ability to see from many different points of view. Julian Hawthorne wrote of his father: "Hawthorne, both by nature and by training, was of a disposition to throw himself imaginatively into the shoes (as the phrase is) of whatever person happened to be his companion." The flowers on the wild rosebush outside the prison door in *The Scarlet Letter* remind the prisoner that "the deep heart of Nature could pity and be kind to him." Throughout his fiction, Hawthorne expresses this kind of sympathy for his fellow human creatures. As Sophia Hawthorne wrote to her mother in 1850, Hawthorne "sees and sympathizes with all human suffering."

This intense feeling for humankind helps to explain the complexity of Hawthorne's vision. There are no easy answers to the questions that critics have raised about Hawthorne's characters because Hawthorne did not see people in terms of black and white. Even the most villainous characters in Hawthorne's major fiction are usually treated with understanding and compassion. . . .

Since Hawthorne does not see people in terms of black and white, there are no "heroes" in his fiction, no superpersons in the tradition of the American myth. Instead, there are only men and women with the strengths and weaknesses of real human beings. . . .

Hawthorne, then, did not subscribe to the individualism that characterized nineteenth-century America. Always sympathetic to the claims of the other in his life and his fiction, he was consequently able to portray woman—the traditional other—as an independent person. Un-American in his denial of the primacy of the self so emphatically asserted by his Transcendentalist neighbors, Hawthorne, despite personal and cultural inhibitions, was acutely aware of the personhood of the female other and was able to create female characters who stand out in American literature as women of substance and individuality. His strong woman is not a shadowy figure outside the reality of life, as was the typical woman created by his American contemporaries, a pretty aeolian harp who existed only to be played upon at will by the stronger winds of masculine vanity. She is a person in herself.

Hawthorne Lets the Patriarchs Win

Louise DeSalvo

Louise DeSalvo is the Jenny Hunter Endowed Scholar for Creative Writing and Literature at Hunter College. A prolific writer, her works include Virginia Woolf's First Voyage *(1980),* Writing as a Way of Healing *(2000), and a series of memoirs, notably* Vertigo *(2002).*

Louise DeSalvo's argument is that Hawthorne, in The Scarlet Letter, *subtly makes Hester a villain who has ruined the lives of those closest to her and escapes the sadistic punishment for adultery historically meted out by Hawthorne's ancestors. According to DeSalvo, the novel paints Dimmesdale and Chillingworth, not Hester, as the real saviors of Hester's daughter, Pearl. Thus, Hawthorne demonizes women and exonerates his unspeakably cruel ancestors, something that he admits, in his introduction, that he plans to do. DeSalvo points out that the evil eagle over the Custom House, who threatens harm to its children (members of the republic) and has cost Hawthorne his job, is female, not male. Likewise, she says, it is the two most powerful men in the Puritan community who suffer the most.*

'Custom-House' which serves as an introduction to and provides a frame for *The Scarlet Letter* was intended by Hawthorne to be a deliberate act of aggression and revenge against the Whigs who were responsible for his dismissal [in 1849] from his post [as surveyor of the Custom House in Salem]. . . .

Although Hawthorne makes it quite clear that he believes that he has been betrayed by *male* politicians, and that he intends to take his revenge upon them, none the less, the image which introduces 'The Custom-House' and dominates it, is the image of the American eagle, which Hawthorne depicts as a negative *female* image. . . .

The Female Eagle

What Hawthorne accomplishes by rendering the national American symbol as female, is, in effect, a shifting of the responsibility and blame for his dismissal from the Custom-House away from the men who were responsible (and, by extension, away from the male-dominated patriarchal political system). Instead, despite his acerbic and rancorous remarks about men in government service, it is clear from this image of the female federal eagle, that, at some deep level, Hawthorne experienced his dismissal as *maternal* rejection, rather than as the result of a male political wrangle. . . .

What the feminist reader of 'The Custom-House' must note is how this image misrepresents political as female, and how it blames a maternal figure for what is, in reality, the action of a male-dominated political machine. . . .

Serving Male History

Hawthorne does not perceive the function of telling his tale as serving the causes of women's history; rather, Hawthorne is using one woman's story to serve the purposes of *male* history, both his own and men in general—a fact that has been overlooked by feminist literary critics. As [past Custom-House surveyor Jonathan] Pue's ghost instructs Hawthorne: '. . . I charge you, in this matter of old Mistress Prynne, give to your predecessor's memory the credit which will be rightfully its due!'

The fundamental assumption about the nature of history that is embedded here is that woman's history is, and ought to be, the *property* of the male historian. Indeed, in the first moments of the novel, as Hester is about to emerge from the prison, Hawthorne uses the word 'narrative' to describe her: just as she is about to emerge from the jail, so is 'our narrative, . . . about to issue from that inauspicious portal'. She is not a character, she is a narrative, and in the language that Hawthorne insists upon, Hester and the narrative are, in fact, the same.

Moreover it is absolutely necessary that this history be presented as if it were authentic *especially if* that account grossly misrepresents woman's history, as the life story of Hester Prynne in *The Scarlet Letter* grossly distorts the fate of women who committed adultery in Puritan New England. In one very important sense, depicting Hester's strength and her resilience in the face of her punishment serves to nullify the effects of such persecution. If Hester could endure, and triumph (as women who were persecuted for adultery surely did not), then the negative consequences of the persecution itself are blunted, and the persecuting fathers rendered less virulent than they in fact were. . . .

Although Hawthorne would have known that Plymouth law decreed two whippings and the wearing of the letters 'AD' on the arm or back of the adulteress, he has omitted the whippings from his romance and has Hester embellish the 'A' into an object of great beauty. . . .

Dimmesdale's Suffering; Hester's Blame

Hawthorne substitutes Dimmesdale's refusal to acknowledge the fact of his paternity (which is surely interesting in light of Hawthorne's biography) and Chillingworth's probing into the secrets of Dimmesdale's heart as greater evils than the evils suffered by those persecuted by Puritan justice! And so, in the context of *The Scarlet Letter*, in a fascinating reversal of the facts of history, Dimmesdale, the representative of the Puritan state and Puritan power in the novel, becomes more sinned against than sinning—he is described as the 'victim . . . for ever on the rack'—and his victimization at the hands of Chillingworth becomes of greater consequence and has more dire results than Hester's punishment! Hawthorne, in his revisionist history, thus substitutes a portrait of a male victim for an accurate portrait of a female victim of the Puritan oligarchy....

As the novel progresses, Hawthorne subtly shifts the blame for what happens to Chillingworth and to Dimmesdale onto the shoulders of Hester. The effect of this is to render Hester completely responsible for the physical, emotional and spiritual well-being of the men in her life. Chillingworth tells her 'Woman, woman, thou art accountable for this' and Dimmesdale repeatedly insists that his salvation is her responsibility: 'Think for me Hester! Thou art strong'. In one very important scene, Chillingworth blames Hester, and not the rigid system of Puritan justice, or his own actions, for Dimmesdale's slow demise: he tells her 'you [Hester] cause him to die daily a living death'; and she accepts the blame for Chillingworth's obsession with revenge—when he asks her who is responsible, she says 'It was myself' just as she accounts herself responsible for Dimmesdale: she becomes 'sensible of the deep injury for which she was responsible to this unhappy man, in permitting him to lie for so many years'. Thus, Hester, the person with the least amount of real power in the novel is made, symbolically, the person with the most power, and the most responsibility for the outcome of the tale....

Diabolical Women

... Hawthorne's principal strategy, at the beginning of the novel itself, is to deflect attention away from the Puritan patriarchs who have voted Hester's punishment, the patriarchs who have made the laws and who enforce them. They scarcely exist as far as the novel is concerned. Rather, as Hester Prynne emerges from the jail, Hawthorne focuses all of his narrative attention, and for several pages, upon the vengeful response of the Puritan *women*. They take 'a peculiar interest in whatever penal infliction might be expected to ensue'. In the novel, it is not the oligarchs, Hawthorne's forebears, who punish, it is the goodwives who demand justice.

> 'Goodwives', said a hard-featured dame of fifty, 'I'll tell ye a piece of my mind. It would be greatly for the public behoof, if we women, being of mature age and church-members in good repute, should have the handling of such malefactresses as this Hester Prynne. What think ye, gossips? If the hussy stood up for judgment before us five, that are now here in a knot to gather, would she come off with such a sentence as the worshipful magistrates have awarded? Marry, I trow not!'

Although Hawthorne appears to be arguing for gender-determined punishment, he is also stating that the male judges who did exist were fairer than any woman would have been. A man in the crowd who overhears the women says 'is there no virtue in woman, save what springs from a wholesome fear of the gallows?' And Hawthorne states that the uglier a woman is, the more vengeance she would exact from criminals: 'the ugliest as well as the most pitiless of these self-constituted judges' says 'This woman has brought shame upon us all and ought to die. Is there not law for it?' All the vengeance at the beginning of the novel has been female; when a beadle finally appears, he seems far less severe than the women; in contrast to their graphic desire to 'put the brand of a hot iron on Hester Prynne's forehead', he simply 'prefigured and represented in his aspect the whole dismal severity of the Puritanic code of law'.

This is a fascinating strategy. Hawthorne denies history by misrepresenting Hester's punishment as if it would have been essentially fair and judicious. Then he argues that if women had had political power, they would have been harsher to adulteresses than his fictional Puritan leaders had been to Hester. Hawthorne therefore creates a romance about judicious Puritan rule which denies the reality of the abuse of power by Puritan rulers, and then he uses the fiction he has created to argue that men are essentially more fair-minded than women would be! This literary strategy, though highly persuasive, is extraordinarily illogical and misleading for Hawthorne draws ethical conclusions about justice being fair-minded if it is male, and vengeful if it is female from a universe which he himself has created, and which is a misrepresentation of historical reality.

The Witch Girl

In the context of the Puritan cosmology developed in *The Scarlet Letter*, Hester Prynne is enormously concerned about what will happen to her child Pearl, as well she should be because the children of miscreants were not treated well in Puritan New England. Throughout the novel, Pearl is repeatedly associated with the devil, with evil, with sin, and with witchcraft: her looks are 'perverse' and 'malicious'; she is an 'imp of evil', 'fiend-like', an 'evil spirit', 'a shadowy reflection of evil', a 'demon offspring', a 'demon-child'; there is a 'fire in her'; her cries are 'a witch's anathemas in some unknown tongue', she is a 'little baggage [who] hath witchcraft in her', there is 'witchcraft in little Pearl's eyes'; she is 'a shadowy reflection of evil', the 'effluence of her mother's lawless passion'; her imaginary playmates are 'the puppets of Pearl's witchcraft'. And Hawthorne makes it clear that she has inherited these tendencies from her mother: although, *in utero*, Pearl's character was at first unblemished, her 'mother's impassioned state had been the medium through which were transmitted to the unborn infant the rays of its mortal life; and, however white and clear originally, they had taken the deep stains of crimson and gold, the fiery lustre, the black shadow'.

The character who is repeatedly associated with Pearl is Mistress Hibbins, who is based upon an actual woman, who, the narrative records, will be accused of witchcraft and who will 'die upon the gallows'. In the forest, Dimmesdale likens Pearl's cries to 'the cankered wrath of an old witch, like Mistress Hibbins'. . . .

The Father as Savior

The process of caring for Pearl, however, leads to Hester's salvation, because through caring for Pearl she avoids becoming a latter-day Anne Hutchinson, and accepts her womanly role, which, according to Hawthorne, is essential if a woman is to be saved. But it is the absent father Dimmesdale who is responsible for Pearl's salvation: as Pearl kisses him at the end of the novel, she feels grief for the first time, and it is this grief, and not her mother's care, which humanizes her:

> Pearl kissed his lips. A spell was broken. The great scene of grief, in which the wild infant bore a part, had developed all her sympathies; and as her tears fell upon her father's cheek, they were the pledge that she would grow up amid human joy and sorrow, nor for ever do battle with the world, but be a woman in it.

This scene effectively obliterates all the years of Hester's mothering. Just as Hawthorne has written his own mother and his wife out of 'The Custom-House', so he writes Hester out of the cause for Pearl's salvation in *The Scarlet Letter*. It is not all the years of Hester's toil which saves Pearl from a life of evil in Puritan New England, or from being persecuted as a witch, like Mistress Hibbins. Rather, Pearl becomes a happy woman because of this single moment that she shares with her father Dimmesdale which unlocks her ability to feel grief. Salvation comes, not as a result of Pearl and Hester working together through the years to make a reasonably good life for themselves despite persecution. No, salvation comes, in Hawthorne's world, from being humanized as a result of feeling sorry for the suffering your *father* has experienced! And even the reprehensible Chillingworth, in leaving Pearl 'a very considerable amount of property, both here and in England' is made even more responsible for Pearl's good fortune, than all the years of Hester's toil as a single parent, raising her child alone. Hawthorne, therefore, privileges the effect of the absent father upon the good fortune of the child over the labour of the present mother.

Chapter 3

Contemporary Perspectives on Women's Issues

The Forced Marriage

John Dougherty and Kirk Johnson

Reporter John Dougherty has extensively investigated the polygamous Mormon communities along the border of Arizona and New Mexico. Kirk Johnson is a staff writer for the New York Times.

Chillingworth admits to Hester that, despite her unfaithfulness, it was he who had done her a great wrong by conspiring with her family in his old age to marry the very young Hester. To this day similar practices persist throughout the world, even to some extent in the United States, especially among religious extremists who, like the Puritans, believe women should be totally controlled by men. Such was the case in a polygamist Mormon sect whose leader, Warren S. Jeffs, was accused in 2006 of forcing the marriage of a fourteen-year-old girl against her wishes. He was charged with and found guilty of being an accomplice to rape. Jeffs faced the possibility of life imprisonment, but his followers—believing their leader to be a prophet to whom God speaks directly—vowed never to relinquish their practices of arranged marriages, underage marriages, and polygamy.

The polygamist Warren S. Jeffs, hailed by his followers as a prophet but denounced by critics as a tyrannical cult leader, was convicted [in St. George, Utah] on Tuesday [September 25, 2007] of being an accomplice to the rape of a 14-year-old church member.

Mr. Jeffs, 51, faces up to life in prison.

The Arranged Marriage

The verdict, by an eight-member state jury here in Washington County, was a vindication of the prosecution's argument—which some experts had thought might be hard to accept—that orchestrating a marriage of a young girl under duress made Mr. Jeffs culpable even though he was not present when the rape occurred.

The girl at the center of the case, who [was] 21 [in September 2007], testified that she was pressed by Mr. Jeffs in early 2001 into a "celestial marriage" she did not want, to a cousin she did not like.

Prosecutors said Mr. Jeffs, the leader of the Fundamentalist Church of Jesus Christ of Latter-day Saints, a Mormon sect with an estimated 10,000 members, knew that the marriage would lead to nonconsensual sex.

The jurors, who began their deliberations on Friday after a week of testimony, announced in a note on Monday that they were deadlocked on one of two charges. The judge, James L. Shumate, pressed them to continue, and then early on Tuesday, for reasons the court did not explain, an alternate juror was substituted for one of the original panel members. A unanimous verdict came a few hours later.

When the verdict was read, about 2:30 p.m., Mountain time, Mr. Jeffs showed no emotion, and his followers who had filled the back rows of the courtroom remained silent.

In the deeply isolated polygamist communities of Hildale, Utah, and nearby Colorado City, Ariz., about an hour southeast of St. George, residents said the verdict would probably just harden the lines of resistance.

"That just makes him all the more the prophet," said Isaac Wyler of Colorado City. Mr. Wyler said Mr. Jeffs ordered him to leave the church in 2004 but gave no reason.

God's Word?

Benjamin Bistline, who left the church voluntarily, said he thought the verdict would shift the balance of church activities—especially marriages—away from the historic base here in southern Utah to more recently established compounds that the leadership tightly controls in Texas, South Dakota and elsewhere.

"They believe that polygamy is God's word, and they will still do under-age marriages," said Mr. Bistline, who has written a history of the sect.

Mr. Jeffs, whose sentencing was scheduled for Nov. 20, still faces state charges in Arizona related to performing under-age or incestuous marriages, and a federal indictment for flight to avoid prosecution. He was arrested in August 2006 near Las Vegas after four months on the F.B.I.'s Most Wanted List.

His trial trial was not about polygamy or religion—at least on the surface. But the decades of bitter relations between the state of Utah, dominated by mainstream Mormons from the Church of Jesus Christ of Latter-day Saints, and Mr. Jeffs's renegade sect [were] never far away.

The mainstream church renounced plural marriage in 1890. In response, some fundamentalist Mormons formed a sect, declaring that the teachings of Mormonism's founder, Joseph Smith, had been forsaken. Mr. Jeffs's lawyer told the jury the trial was really about that old conflict, and about the freedom of religion—a deeply resonant theme here.

The prosecutor, Brock Belnap, said religion was not only irrelevant, but also a deliberate distraction that he said the defense was trying to inject to cloud jurors' judgment. He said after the verdict that he expected an appeal.

One of Mr. Jeffs's lawyers, Walter F. Bugden, said they would appeal.

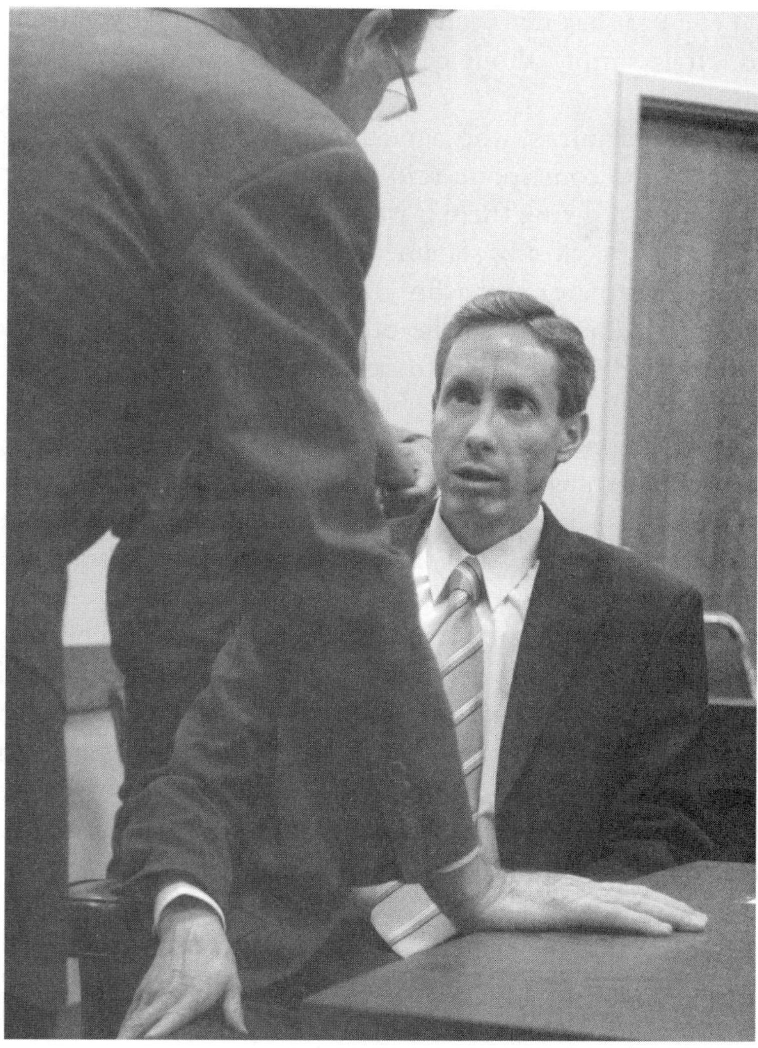

Warren Jeffs, head of the Fundamentalist Church of Jesus Christ of Latter-day Saints, confers with his defense attorney September 24th, 2007. Jeffs was charged and found guilty of forcing a fourteen-year-old follower's marriage to and rape by her nineteen-year-old cousin. Jud Burkett/AFP/Getty Images.

Abuse, Not Religion

The girl in the case, who was identified by the court as Jane Doe, said in a statement read outside the courthouse that the case was not about vengeance.

"The trial has not been about religion nor a vendetta," she said. "It is simply about child abuse and preventing further abuse."

The eight jurors, who agreed to be interviewed by reporters inside the courtroom, said Mr. Belnap's closing statement was crucial in giving them a roadmap of the law.

"It was the closing statement that did it," said Rachel Karimi, the alternate juror who joined the panel Tuesday morning. Ms. Karimi, 28, and the other jurors, declined to discuss the dismissed juror except to say she had also favored conviction.

Some jurors said they were convinced that Mr. Jeffs had overwhelming power over the lives in his community—a conclusion crucial to reaching the verdict. One juror, Lynn Maxwell, 40, said, "He was not there to help her when things went wrong, and she was raped."

The jurors said they also dismissed the defense argument that the focus on Mr. Jeffs was unfair because others in the church could have done something to help. The girl's mother and her sister to whom she went for help would have faced repercussions, the jurors said.

"He was the only one who had the power," said another juror, Diedre Shaw, 32.

The Single Mother

Ruth Sidel

Ruth Sidel is professor of sociology at Hunter College. Her books include Keeping Women and Children Last: America's War on the Poor *(1998) and* On Her Own: Growing Up in the Shadow of the American Dream *(1990).*

Ruth Sidel's research, based on a series of interviews with single mothers, has led her to the conclusion that their lives have been made much harder by the rise in social conservatism that began during the Reagan administration. Sidel argues that the damning of single mothers (by presidents and other politicians) has resulted in reductions of badly needed government assistance. Because they must be mothers and fathers to their offspring, single mothers, especially those who are poor, have labored under heavy burdens, both economic and psychological. The interviews convinced Sidel that one persistent problem for single mothers is the perpetuation of negative stereotypes. According to Sidel, political leaders also burden single mothers with guilt, holding them responsible for all of society's ills.

The denigration and demonization of single mothers has deep roots in American culture. Mothers without husbands have been looked upon with suspicion and hostility since the time of the earliest settlers. Today's concerns about the weakening of the traditional family and about related issues such as single motherhood, divorce, sexual permissiveness, teenage pregnancy, and abortion have formed a central theme in American society for generations. Both the early Settlement Laws and the Colonial Poor Laws of seventeenth-century America punished husbandless women and unwed mothers, differentiating between the "deserving" and the "undeserving." During the early years of the twentieth century, programs to help the poor stated that only "fit and worthy" women would receive help; these generally were white widows.

Socioeconomics and the Single Mother

The recent period of intensified concern about single motherhood was spurred by the ascendancy of conservative ideology in the United States as marked by the election of Ronald Reagan as president. Rapid social change during the 1970s and 1980s—increasing numbers of single mothers, especially women having children outside marriage; a significant increase in teenage pregnancy and birth; a continuing high divorce rate; and fundamental changes in the roles and status of women—contributed to the anxiety about social issues. Reagan's infamous labeling of poor women as "welfare queens" was accompanied by significant cutbacks in essential social services, particularly for poor women and children. In the early 1980s Medicaid, Aid to Families with Dependent Children, the food stamp program, maternal and child health services, and day care were all slashed. These cutbacks increased the number of poor people and had a particularly devastating impact on female-headed families. Consequently, during this period there was a significant increase in both the "feminization" and the "minoritization" of poverty.

Stereotyped and Stigmatized

Since the early 1990s, single mothers have continued to be systematically stereotyped and stigmatized. Poor single mothers have once again been vilified as being lazy, irresponsible, dependent, deviant, and, above all, living off the hard work of others. Single mothers, particularly those who have children outside of marriage, have been blamed for virtually all the nation's social problems—the "breakdown of the family," the crime rate, drug and alcohol addiction, illiteracy, homelessness, poverty, and students' poor academic performance. Perhaps the most denigrating and dehumanizing attacks on single mothers occurred in 1995 on the floor of the U.S. House of Representatives when, as part of an effort to reduce the money spent on social welfare programs, two members of Congress compared welfare recipients to animals. This campaign was fueled by conservative Republicans, spearheaded by [then-congressman] Newt Gingrich and buttressed by the work of the social scientist Charles Murray, who labeled out-of-wedlock births "the single most important problem of our time" as he railed against the "culture of illegitimacy." Bill Clinton seemed to support the negative view of welfare recipients when he made his now-famous promise in 1991, during the presidential campaign, to "put an end to welfare as we know it."

In 1992, the then vice president, Dan Quayle, set off a firestorm by condemning Murphy Brown, the central character in a popular television sitcom, for having a baby outside of marriage. . . .

In a speech in March 1995, Newt Gingrich, then the Speaker of the House of Representatives, recommended returning to the values, norms, and social sanctions of Victorian England in order to modify antisocial behavior: "They [the Victorians] reduced the number of children born out of wedlock almost by 50 percent. They changed the whole momentum of their society. They didn't do it through a new bureaucracy. They did it by reestablishing values, by moral leadership, and by being willing to look at people in the face and say, 'You should be ashamed when you get drunk in public; you ought to be ashamed if you're a drug addict.'" Of course, Gingrich was also saying that American society must send the message that people should be ashamed to have children out of wedlock and that we should not be afraid of using shame to change behavior. One is reminded of Hester Prynne in *The*

Scarlet Letter, stepping out of prison into the Massachusetts marketplace with that "mark of shame upon her bosom," so that "she will be a living sermon against sin, until the ignominous letter will be engraved upon her tombstone." . . .

The Economic Question

Thus, while life has become increasingly difficult and complex [since the mid-1990s], as more and more jobs have disappeared, as those that remain often pay far less than a living wage, as millions must survive without essentials such as health insurance, and as the gap between rich and poor widens to Gatsbyesque proportions, families have largely been left to fend for themselves. Mother-only families have not only had to withstand a relentless barrage of criticism but have also seen social and financial support diminish significantly.

Who exactly are single mothers today? First, it must be emphasized that women become single mothers in a variety of ways: through separation from their husbands, through divorce, through widowhood, and through having children outside of marriage. No one scenario or set of circumstances explains the diverse, complex lives of single mothers. It must be stressed as well that millions of single mothers never intended to live their lives raising their children without the support of a partner. When they find themselves alone and in charge of their family, many recognize for the first time the harsh reality of being a single parent in the United States today.

The dramatic change in American family structure over the past half century has been well documented. The percentage of women with children under 18 not living with a husband rose from 10 percent in 1940 to 24 percent in 2000. The sharpest increase occurred between 1960 and 1990; since then the percentage has remained stable. Not only the statistics but the causes of the increase in single-parent families have changed significantly. During the first half of the twentieth

A 1940s factory worker holds her child in her arms. Recent research conducted by Ruth Sidel shows that the withdrawal of badly needed government assistance for single mothers results from society's stereotyping of these women. H. Armstrong Roberts/Retrofile/Hulton Archive/Getty Images.

century the primary cause of single parenthood was parental death; by the end of the century most absent parents were living, but they were living elsewhere. . . .

Single Mothers Speak for Themselves

This study is a realistic, detailed examination of the lives of single mothers from their perspectives, intended to correct the harsh, hostile, often erroneous, sometimes venomous stereotypes about single mothers endlessly reiterated by pundits, politicians, and members of the media. Bizarre examples of highly unusual behavior are all too often put forth and deplored as though they were the norm and then are taken as typical of all single mothers. Moreover, these often outlandish examples are presented as the true experiences of the entire group, used to reinforce the prevailing stereotypes and to formulate social policy. This book examines the real lives of a variety of single mothers: how they grew up, how they became the sole or primary caregivers of their children, how becoming a single parent disrupted their lives and affected them, and how they subsequently rebuilt their social, emotional, and economic world. . . .

Many of these mothers also showed a powerful and often courageous resilience as well as the strength and ability to find new ways out of their exceedingly difficult and often wrenching situations. After they entered the world of single motherhood, the women all had to face putting their lives back together—making new living arrangements, dealing with financial issues, balancing work and nurturing, finding adequate child care and after-school care, figuring out the role of extended family and friends, exploring the often delicate problem of having a social life, and sometimes dealing with their own self-doubt, feelings of inadequacy, and sadness. They all were forced to grapple with these issues regardless of how they became single mothers. To be sure, more affluent women have considerably more choice in solving these fundamental problems, but they too usually agonized about how to handle it all, about what was the "right" path for them. . . .

Surviving

The women who speak out in this book are younger, older, black, white, Latina. They have become single mothers by many routes. Among the separated and divorced, some have been left by their husbands and others have themselves left the relationship. Some have been physically or emotionally abused; others have not. Some are struggling financially; for others money is not their primary concern. But they have all experienced significant disruption in their lives, and this book examines how these women have dealt and continue to deal with wrenching changes in their hopes, dreams, and expectations and how they are rebuilding their lives in an exceedingly hostile social, economic, and political environment. This is also a study of strength, of resilience, of courage, and of support. Some of the women have heroically refashioned their lives and are clearly walking down a path uncharted by anyone in their immediate environment; for others their lives are still a work in progress. Whatever their experiences, they cannot be reduced to a simplistic stereotype, an "idée fixe," or a "controlling image." These women, their children, and their complex relationships cannot be neatly summed up, characterized by some preexisting formula; the rote predictions of their futures (often ominous) are rarely accurate.

Still Quiet and Submissive

John Hooper and Jo Revill; John Hooper and Tania Branigan

John Hooper, who reports for the London-based newspapers the Guardian *and the* Observer, *worked from Rome on these two stories. Jo Revill, co-reporter on the first story, is Whitehall editor at the* Observer. *Tania Branigan, who wrote the second story with Hooper, is a political correspondent for the* Guardian.

Two articles on a papal decree reflect a continuing repressive attitude toward women. The first article focuses on the role played by then Cardinal Joseph Ratzinger (who became Pope in 2005) in the writing of the report, which declares that woman's God-given nature leads her to be quiet, humble and faithful. She is supposed to listen, welcome, praise, wait, and deal with the practical, not the abstract.

The second article focuses on the Roman Catholic Church's attacks on feminism, which the church sees as undermining woman's rightful maternal role, heretically urging the blessing of female priests, promoting wrongheaded ideas of sexuality, and assuring couples that birth control is acceptable. One feminist author announced that the Pope was belittling woman's work in the public arena. Another issue raised by the report is the extent of the differences between the sexes and the roles to which women are restricted because of those perceived differences.

The Vatican yesterday [July 31, 2004] depicted what it claimed were women's characteristic traits: 'Listening, welcoming, humility, faithfulness, praise and waiting.'

In its most important statement on the role of women in almost a decade, the Roman Catholic Church said these virtues of the Virgin Mary were ones that women displayed 'with particular intensity and naturalness'.

The 37-page statement, published in full yesterday, was written by the Pope's top theologian, Cardinal Joseph Ratzinger. As a statement of official doctrine, it would have been read, and very likely amended, by the Pope [John Paul II] himself before publication.

A Controversial Edict on Women

The document, which will prompt a fierce debate about the attributes of women, added: 'Although a certain type of feminist rhetoric makes demands "for ourselves", women preserve the deep intuition of the goodness in their lives of those actions that elicit life, and contribute to the growth and protection [of others]. This intuition is linked to women's physical capacity to give life. Whether lived out or remaining potential, this capacity is a reality that structures the female personality in a profound way.'

In his 'Letter to the Bishops of the Catholic Church on the Collaboration of Men and Women in the Church and in the World', Ratzinger takes aim at 'currents of thought that are often at variance with the authentic advancement of women'. Chief among these is a tendency to 'emphasise strongly, conditions of subordination in order to give rise to antagonism'.

It implied that 'women, in order to be themselves, must make themselves the adversaries of men'. Such confrontational thinking was 'leading to harmful confusion . . . which has its most immediate and lethal effects in the structure of the family'.

Gender war also encouraged a perilous blurring of the distinctions. 'To avoid the domination of one sex or the other, their differences tend to be denied, viewed as mere effects of historical and cultural conditioning.'

Such a view ignored qualities that arose from a woman's unique ability to give birth. This 'allows her to acquire maturity very quickly, and gives a sense of the seriousness of life and of its responsibilities. A sense and a respect for what is concrete develop in her, opposed to abstractions which are so often fatal for the existence of individuals and society,' says the first high-level pronouncement on gender issues since the Pope's 1995 'Letter to Women'.

Ratzinger uses the document to argue that, because they have something unique to contribute, 'women should be present in the world of work and in the organisation of society'.

Mixed Reactions

The comments drew a mixed reaction from feminists and women writers. Erin Pizzey, founder of the international women's refuge movement, said: 'I don't think the Catholic Church, whose priests and bishops cannot marry, is in a position to make such statements. It is one of the most emotionally illiterate organisations I know, and it needs to put its own house in order first.'

But Catherine Pepinster, editor of Catholic paper The Tablet, said the comments would resonate with many women. 'For feminists to rubbish it is a knee-jerk response. It does make a distinction between the sexes, but it also points out that women have a big role to play in society.'

Tory MP [Member of Parliament] Ann Widdecombe said that the statement seemed to her a long-overdue assessment of women's roles.

'For those of us involved in the women's movement of the Seventies, our aim was to give us equal opportunities. It wasn't that we would become men. Instead of civilising the world, what we have done is create a ladette culture. It's true we have certain characteristics that we can bring to the world that are valuable, and shouldn't be submerged.'

However, combining work and family has 'characteristics different from those in the case of men', says the document, which argues for a 'just valuing of the work of women within the family'. Ratzinger does not say how this is to be done, but it is clear he sees it as a way of encouraging women to spend as much time as possible in the home.

The Pope will call on leaders of the Roman Catholic church today to attack feminist ideologies which assert that men and women are fundamentally the same.

The Vatican is concerned that this belief is eroding what it regards as women's maternal vocation. But a paper on the subject which is due to be published today [July 31, 2004]—the Vatican's third major pronouncement on women's role in the quarter century of John Paul's papacy—has drawn scornful criticism from feminists and academics.

Gender Differences

According to a leaked extract, the document accuses feminists of "blurring the biological difference between man and woman".

But it is also understood to break new ground by appealing to governments to give help to women so they can cope with their broader modern responsibilities.

It emerged yesterday that the Vatican itself had taken a further step towards incorporating women into the previously all-male leadership of the Roman Catholic church. A nun, who was not named in Italian media reports, was said to be working as a high-level aide to the Pope's "foreign minister", Archbishop Giovanni Lajolo.

The statement of doctrine on gender issues is the first serious attempt by the Vatican to come to grips with a world of working women. But it is just as clearly intended to prevent any erosion of the church's resolute opposition to gay marriage, the incorporation of women into the priesthood, and trends in gender studies which the Pope has damned as "misleading conceptions of sexuality".

The Vatican's sights are trained in particular on the view that while people's sex is anatomically determined their gender identity and roles are entirely a product of conditioning. In a letter to bishops on the participation of men and women in the church and the world, the Pope's chief theological spokesman, the German cardinal Joseph Ratzinger, stresses, as the pontiff has done on several occasions, that the book of Genesis is unambiguous on this point.

The letter was drawn up inside Cardinal Ratzinger's Vatican "ministry", the Congregation for the Doctrine of the Faith. However, as a statement of doctrine, it would not have been sent for publication without the consent of the Pope.

The Vatican's letter acknowledges that the emancipation of women, which the pontiff applauded in his earliest pronouncements on the subject, has given them a vastly increased presence in the labour market.

Recent decades have seen a plunge in birth and fertility rates, particularly in the Roman Catholic heartland of southern Europe, as women struggle to combine jobs with their traditional roles as mothers, homemakers and carers.

A Breakdown in Values

Church representatives have argued that this is symptomatic of a breakdown in values, and particularly a greater selfishness among young couples more interested in consumer goods than creating life. Feminists have long held that it is a result of the reluctance of men to share household tasks and the failure of governments to provide adequate support for families.

Cardinal Ratzinger's document appears to have embraced implicitly the feminist view on this point, though in language unlikely to win over many feminists.

According to the leaked extract in the German tabloid Bild Zeitung, his letter to bishops calls on governments to "create conditions that enable women not to neglect their family duties when they enter into a job".

Dr Helena Cronin, an evolutionary psychologist at the London School of Economics, said: "It's absolutely true that we are different, in a variety of ways." She said that in all mammals, females showed a greater propensity to caring for the young than males did. But she added: "That's not saying that women have no other vocations, or that they should be devoted [to motherhood]."

The feminist author Natasha Walter questioned whether there were essential differences between men and women at all.

"We have centuries and centuries of acculturation towards a 'vocation' of maternity, and men have only had a couple of generations of acculturation towards active paternity. Until we encourage men [to do more] it's too early to call on whether there are innate differences. The weight of tradition is so strong that it precludes the freedom to choose."

However, Eva Figes, whose book Patriarchal Attitudes was one of the major works of feminism's "second wave" in the 70s, said: "I have always thought men and women were different—we have better linguistic skills, for instance—but it wasn't politic to say so when I was writing 30 years ago."

She added: "The trouble is we all know the Pope's opinions on issues such as abortion and contraception.

"There is another agenda there: he will think maternity is more important than public life. I don't see why women should not have both—and it should be their choice."

"GodMen" in a Defeminized Church

Paul T. Coughlin

Paul T. Coughlin is the host of a talk show on Christian radio, a lecturer, and key founder of a group called GodMen.

Paul T. Coughlin has a view of women that is revealed primarily in his castigation of womanly qualities, which he claims have polluted the church and the family. Jesus, he writes, was not meek and mild, as the "feminized" church has presented him. Jesus was a tough, aggressive warrior who would have denounced the "Christian nice guy." Although Coughlin acknowledges the unfair and unequal treatment of women before the rise of the feminist movement, he believes that women have inappropriately taken over the domestic sphere and that it is now men who are the victims of gender discrimination.

The church, partially with noble motive, encourages men to deny vital parts of their masculine composition, often stored in their cooling hearts, in order to shore up our culture's crumbling families and in doing so combat our incredible rates of divorce, child neglect, and related ills.

Many thinking people, more conservative than liberal, now look back with regret upon the feminist movement and its sexual revolution. The 1960s in America helped create one of the greatest periods of gender confusion in history, and both sexes bear the blame. . . .

The Church's Strong Medicine to Men

The sexual revolution's destruction of the nuclear family is now a historical reality. Equally established is how the church fought back—one of only a handful of cultural institutions

Paul T. Coughlin, *No More Christian Nice Guy*. Ada, MI: Bethany House, 2005.

with enough guts to do so—by telling entire generations of men to take their responsibility and duty more seriously. This, in fact, has been the primary cry of churches for more than four decades: *Men, focus only upon your domestic responsibilities.* A Christian man has been told for decades that his wife's priorities should be his priorities, and the result is astounding: Evangelical wives now report higher levels of sex-life satisfaction than any other group. How evangelical men wish this was true for them as well.

Christians and non-Christians alike should be grateful for this redemptive, heroic mission that has proven to be both noble and problematic. It came during a desperate time and from a church that enmeshed itself in the toil of life even as some other groups applauded the devastation, calling it progress. The church had little time to worry about the unforeseen fallout from this over-corrective message. Fighting a devouring cancer, it has used a powerful antidote, one with an unintended side effect: We are over-domesticated. Men are dying inside because we've ignored a critical portion of our heart, a vital source of masculine power, courage, and bravery; in being "nice and responsible," it's as if we're living by a creed of "Let's not make things any worse than we already have." . . .

The Domestic Cult

Christian men *have* made amazing progress as fathers and husbands; the bad news is, in the process they've lost an integral aspect of themselves through over-domestication. Worse, they are sometimes shamed for possessing such masculine inclinations as the desire to spend time with other men and the embracing of a competitive spirit. Your average Christian guy also lives under the weight of unattainable domestic expectations put upon him by a church that leans heavily against his disposition. It's time that masculine feelings, wants, and aspirations are taken into consideration as well. It's time for a great female awakening, what [conservative radio talk-show host] Dr. Laura [Schlessinger] humorously refers to as "the proper care and feeding of husbands."

To everyone's detriment, Christian men are like poodles—once an admirable hunting dog that's been so housebroken it's now afraid to get its feet wet. Christian Nice Guys are indoctrinated to do nothing that messes with domestic tranquility. Furthermore, in most sermons, home life is portrayed as the near exclusive domain of women, who define right and wrong through feminine sensibilities and often don't understand (and, consequently, discount) masculine ways. If you examine a CNG's home, for instance, chances are you'll find that he didn't have much say in its decoration. He gets the garage (and *maybe* the den or the office) and then is commanded to keep it clean. . . .

When authentic domestic tranquility, then, is *not* achieved, men are left with no real advocate within the church; as a result, God's alleged will for our lives has become far more female-oriented (domestic) than what the Bible actually says. Throw in the strangely popular notion that somehow women are intrinsically more moral and spiritual, and you've got a real mess on your hands.

I don't know how many homilies, designed to *relieve* tension between the sexes, I've sat through where the preacher depicted women in almost supernatural terms, creating even *more* tension. These ministers have redesigned our placement in the spiritual realm with God at the top, angels next, followed by women, then finally us male cretins. When women are described as a nearly exclusive source of spiritual insight and moral understanding, the warning to CNGs is clear: Don't disagree with her, don't cross her, don't disturb her groove. I couldn't help but think, *If they're truly gifted in that way, why shouldn't they lead?*

Don't we realize that such a message can easily lead to nothing better than spiritual arrogance and a misuse of power? And if it does, will that be the husband's fault too?

I call this genderism, and it's akin to racism. Skinheads and neo-Nazis order their moral hierarchy of people based upon ethnicity, contending that some races are better than others; their prejudice offends all but a radical fringe. Yet simultaneously we let another such sinister perspective slip by us and into us at church, a prejudice veneered by a spiritual façade: We categorize human virtue based upon gender, which is morally neutral—men and women are *equally* fallen, sinful, and forgivable. Like racism, genderism leads to mockery, assault, bias, and injustice. And, like racism, genderism strips people—men, in this case—of identity and dignity. . . .

Women, Men, and Spirituality

What does any of this have to do with women being intrinsically more spiritual? The placement of this gender-based divide into our spirituality, and the related granting of de facto superiority to women over men, illustrates how the church's pervasive genderism is spiritually and emotionally dangerous to the docile, subservient Christian husband who, under such weight, is not inclined ever to confront or question his wife on anything, no matter how lovingly. For many, the experience of genderism's heavy-handedness goes back even farther than their adult life in the church, for many evangelical mothers misguidedly attempt to drive God-given masculine desires out of their young boys.

How did we come largely to embrace genderism against the witness of scriptural teaching? The Bible constantly addresses spirituality and morality; *nowhere* does it state or imply that either women or men are more spiritual or moral than the other. I'm with the apostle Paul on this one: *All are equal in Christ Jesus. . . .*

The Husband Is Always to Blame

Domestic happiness is a delicate matter made worse in books for Christian men by messages that appear reasonable but don't work in real life. For example, though a husband has some influence regarding his wife's happiness (and vice versa), this influence has been overblown. A CNG husband has been enslaved to the notion that if his wife isn't happy—for whatever reason—then it's up to him to fix it. In fact, he's at fault if he doesn't, even though the idea that one person can actually make another happy contradicts real-life experience. How I wish more women would admit that this sort of thinking is a tyranny for men. . . .

Men are finally pushing back. After reading my related articles in *New Man* magazine, guys have told me they've had it with men being blamed for any problem that takes place in marriage and in society in general. One particularly frustrated man lamented: "Men are responsible for every problem in their homes, even when it's out of their control. If tragedy hits their home, they are told that the reason why is because they didn't lead like they should and that they didn't pray enough. It's unfair, and it's not even in the Bible!"

I've been in the church for more than twenty-five years now. I've had long talks there, I've had other long talks over dinner in members' homes, and I've noticed some patterns. For one, some of the Christian wives say nothing about God personally—going to church is about family, about family values. I'm all for family values, don't get me wrong. But I'm left with the sinking feeling that their real motive for going to church is so that man of theirs will "get his act together." If this is true, church isn't about an intimate relationship with God, but about keeping Christian men in line, which is to say, domesticated, by female standards. Men will start going back to church when this mindset is called what it is: manipulation. . . .

America's Feminized Faith

America's feminized Christianity has a drawn-out and somewhat complicated history. . . .

Because women were seen [in the 1700s] as morally and spiritually superior, the societal prizing of their influence became imbalanced; this, of course, included the church. . . . No wonder this was the time where with increasing frequency we find Jesus described almost entirely in terms such as "pious and pure, loving and merciful, meek and humble." After all, if a society buys the fallacy that *women* are morally and spiritually superior, then eventually Christ must undergo drastic cultural hormone therapy too. We saw earlier that one objector to this nonsense was Charles Haddon Spurgeon, who said, "There has got abroad a notion, somehow, that if you become a Christian you must sink your manliness and turn milksop." . . .

During the 1900s, Christians married Christ's male gender to a heavy dose of femininity. Women were creating a version of Jesus that they wanted men to copy. . . . Such a person would *not* garner allegiance from one or be followed by men, in his day or ours. He would garner their irritation. . . .

Such feminization was met with a backlash during the 1800s and early 1900s, when influential men such as novelist Henry James complained that "the whole generation is womanized; the masculine tone is passing out of the world." No wonder a 1920 YMCA study determined that U.S. churches were only one-third male: "Roughly, three million men were missing from the pews."

At long last, progress began to manifest itself. A more accurate and masculine Christ was allowed out of the cultural closet as the twentieth century advanced. . . .

This progress continued only until it was beat back by the feminist revolt, the negative aspects of which we still battle today. Feminism may have started off seeking equality for women, but it soon degenerated into attacking the very soul of men, shaming men for their "abusive" and destructive nature. . . .

When we're free from the myths that Jesus is the Supreme Nice Guy, that the Father is a cosmic teddy bear, and that the Holy Spirit is a docile, breezy presence, men will find the church more compelling and relevant, and Christian Nice Guys will begin to see the world more clearly.

Hester's Powerful Progeny

Karen Breslau

Karen Breslau, San Francisco bureau chief for Newsweek, *has covered such important stories as the fall of the Berlin Wall and the civil war in Yugoslavia.*

When Hawthorne wrote The Scarlet Letter, *women in the United States could not vote, much less follow a calling in government. A woman's place was in the home. But in 2007 a woman was a leading candidate for president of the United States, a woman was Speaker of the U.S. House of Representatives, and nine women were state governors. Women governors are routinely regarded by their constituencies as more effective, courageous, and fair than their male counterparts. In 2006 Janet Napolitano, a Democrat, was re-elected governor of the majority-Republican state of Arizona by a landslide, and she has had the courage and clout to veto many bills passed by Democrats and Republicans alike. She has also successfully taken on the federal government on occasion. In similar fashion, Alaska governor Sarah Palin has challenged corruption and greed in her state's powerful oil industry.*

In 1998, voters in a focus group were asked to close their eyes and imagine what a governor should look like. "They automatically pictured a man," says Barbara Lee, whose foundation promoting women's political advancement sponsored the survey. "The kind you see in those portraits hanging in statehouse hallways." They most certainly didn't visualize Alaska Gov. Sarah Palin, a former beauty-pageant winner, avid hunter, snowmobiler and mother of four who was elected to her state's highest office last November. Or Arizona Gov. Janet Napolitano, a badge-wielding former federal prosecutor and

Karen Breslau, "Now This Is Woman's Work," *Newsweek*, October 15, 2007, pp. 66, 68.

onetime attorney for Anita Hill [the law professor who famously testified in 1991 that U.S. Supreme Court Justice Clarence Thomas had sexually harrassed her] who has redefined the debate over illegal immigration in her state.

More Governors than Ever

While [2007]'s political buzz has been about Hillary Clinton's run for the White House and Nancy Pelosi's ascension to Speaker of the House, women leaders like Palin, a Republican, and Napolitano, a Democrat, have gained significant power in the lives of millions of Americans at the state level. In addition to Alaska and Arizona, Michigan, Kansas, Washington, Hawaii, Connecticut, Louisiana and Delaware elected or re-elected women governors in the last year. That's a total of nine, the highest number to serve simultaneously. And next year women candidates will run for the statehouse in North Carolina and Indiana. A decade ago only 16 women in U.S. history had served as governor (four of them were appointed to replace their dead husbands or other ill-fated male predecessors). Today that number stands at 29. "The best way for people to believe in women as competent executives is by actually watching them govern," says Lee. "They find them likable, strong and effective."

New research shows that voters give female governors significantly higher marks than their male counterparts on such qualities as honesty, cooperation and caring—as well as toughness. And at a time when the national debate has become poisonously partisan, governors like Napolitano, 49, and Palin, 43, are making their mark with a pragmatic, postpartisan approach to solving problems, a style that works especially well with the large numbers of independent voters in their respective states.

Napolitano vetoed 127 bills proposed by Republican lawmakers during her first term. But she also went on to approve tax cuts opposed by some of her fellow Democrats while winning Republican support for her pet project, funding all-day kindergarten. She was the first governor of either party to demand that the federal government live up to its constitutional responsibility to secure her state's border with Mexico while at the same time fending off conservatives' efforts to deny social services to illegal immigrants. In 2006, President George W. Bush traveled to the Arizona border, where he publicly praised Napolitano's policies. She won re-election in a landslide, and in a state where Republicans still hold the majority. "Arizonans don't wake up saying, 'I'm a blue person' or 'I'm a red person,'" Napolitano tells Newsweek. "They wake up saying, 'How is the governor dealing with my freeway problem, my school problem, my whatever issue it is of the day?'"

Challenging Big Oil

In Alaska, Palin is challenging the dominant, sometimes corrupting, role of oil companies in the state's political culture. "The public has put a lot of faith in us," says Palin during a meeting with lawmakers in her downtown Anchorage office, where—as if to drive the point home—the giant letters on the side of the ConocoPhillips skyscraper fill an entire wall of windows. "They're saying, 'Here's your shot, clean it up.'" For Palin, that has meant tackling the cozy relationship between the state's political elite and the energy industry that provides 85 percent of Alaska's tax revenues—and distancing herself from fellow Republicans, including the state's senior U.S. senator, Ted Stevens, whose home was recently searched by FBI agents looking for evidence in an ongoing corruption investigation. (Stevens has denied any wrongdoing.) But even as she tackles Big Oil's power, Palin has transformed her own family's connections to the industry into a political advantage. Her husband, Todd, is a longtime employee of BP, but, as Palin points out, the "First Dude" is a blue-collar "sloper," a fieldworker on the North Slope, a cherished occupation in the state. "He's not in London making the decisions whether to build a gas line."

In an interview with Newsweek, Palin said it's time for Alaska to "grow up" and end its reliance on pork-barrel spending. Shortly after taking office, Palin canceled funding for the "Bridge to Nowhere," a $330 million project that Stevens helped champion in Congress. The bridge, which would have linked the town of Ketchikan to an island airport, had come to symbolize Alaska's dependence on federal handouts. Rather than relying on such largesse, says Palin, she wants to prove Alaska can pay its own way, developing its huge energy wealth in ways that are "politically and environmentally clean."

Frontier Women

It's no coincidence that two of the nation's most popular women governors come from frontier states (Arizona and Alaska were the 48th and 49th, respectively, to join the Union) without established social orders that tend to block women from power. In Washington (the 42nd state), Gov. Christine Gregoire and both U.S. senators are women, a trifecta yet to be achieved by any other state. As women reach these top jobs, even more women enter the political pipeline. "When voters perceive things are bad, they expect a woman candidate to come in and create change," says Debbie Walsh of the Center for American Women and Politics at Rutgers University. "Voters give them license not to fit the mold."

They also are willing to embrace women in nontraditional roles as protectors or enforcers of the public interest. Napolitano, like Gregoire and Gov. Jennifer Granholm of Michigan, served as her state's attorney general. Granholm and Gregoire made national reputations helping the states win a record $200 billion settlement against the tobacco industry in the 1990s. Napolitano prosecuted human-smuggling rings as a U.S. attorney in the Clinton administration, and as state attorney general sued long-distance provider Qwest for consumer fraud. "It's a very authentic role for women to do that kind of caretaking and say, 'I am going to look after your interests,'"

Former Democratic presidential candidate Senator Hillary Rodham Clinton addresses her supporters. At the time Hawthorne wrote The Scarlet Letter, *women in the United States were unable to vote, much less run for office.* AP Images.

says Walsh. "What makes them formidable as candidates is experience as the chief law-enforcement officer for their state, a role that exudes strength. Which is always the question asked about a woman. 'Is she strong enough? Is she tough enough?'"

Who's in Charge?

It's a question Napolitano doesn't bother with much anymore. Sitting in her Phoenix statehouse office, decorated with sports memorabilia, law-enforcement badges and the flags of Arizona National Guard units serving in Iraq, Napolitano is surrounded by a cluster of public-safety experts, reviewing preparations for next winter's Super Bowl, which will be played near Phoenix. "Who's in charge?" she demands, jabbing at an impossibly complex organizational chart listing dozens of law-enforcement agencies. "Who do I call if something goes wrong?" That practical approach has impressed lawmakers, even if they don't agree with her on the issues. "Her door is always open," says State Sen. Tom O'Halleran, a Republican, who has clashed with Napolitano over legislation but is also impressed by her negotiating skills. "She's not stuck to an ideology."

Although she has been in office less than a year, Palin, too, earns high marks from lawmakers on the other side of the aisle. During a debate earlier this year over a natural-gas bill, State Senate Minority Leader Beth Kerttula was astounded when she and another Democrat went to see the new governor to lay out their objections. "Not only did we get right in to see her," says Kerttula, "but she asked us back twice—we saw her three times in 10 hours, until we came up with a solution." Next week in Juneau, Alaska lawmakers will meet to overhaul the state's system for taxing oil companies—a task Palin says was tainted last year by an oil-industry lobbyist who pleaded guilty to bribing lawmakers. Kerttula doesn't expect to agree with the freshman governor on every step of the complex undertaking. But the minority leader looks forward to exploiting one backroom advantage she's long waited for. "I finally get to go to the restroom and talk business with the governor," she says. "The guys have been doing this for centuries." And who says that's not progress?

For Further Discussion

1. Critics continue to disagree about fundamental ideas in *The Scarlet Letter*. One important matter of contention can be seen in the interpretation of Hester herself. Is Hawthorne primarily sympathetic with her or primarily critical of her? See the views of Louise DeSalvo and Nina Baym. Choose a stance and have a debate on the question, feeling free to form your own opinion and to disagree with the critics regarding this and other issues.
2. Contrast Hawthorne's view of women in early America, as it is discussed by Joyce W. Warren, with Karen Breslau's reportage of women's power today.
3. Many people see woman's vocation as a critical issue in *The Scarlet Letter*. Is Hester able to fulfill her vocation? See Ken Egan Jr., David S. Reynolds, and Frederick Newberry.
4. Motherhood is a prominent issue in *The Scarlet Letter*, whether one is considering the possible influence of Hawthorne's mother on his writing of the novel or Hester's role as mother. What does the novel have to say about motherhood? See John L. Idol Jr. and Gloria Erlich.
5. Explore the Puritan church's attitude toward woman's nature, referring to Leland S. Person and Kristin Herzog. Compare and contrast that with Paul Coughlin's 2005 view of women and their place in the church and the Roman Catholic Church's stance in John Hooper's reports.
6. In a peculiar way, *The Scarlet Letter* is focused on the issues of marriage and the family. What attitudes does the novel project regarding these institutions? Consult Alison Easton and others. How do attitudes about marriage and the family resonate today? See Ruth Sidel, John Hooper and associates, and John Dougherty and Kirk Johnson.

For Further Reading

Louisa May Alcott, *Work: A Story of Experience*. Boston: Roberts Brothers, 1873.

Charlotte Brontë, *Jane Eyre*. London: Smith, Elder, and Co., 1847.

Kate Chopin, *The Awakening*. Chicago: H.S. Stone and Co., 1899.

Theodore Dreiser, *Sister Carrie*. New York: Doubleday, Page, and Co., 1900.

Fanny Fern, *Ruth Hall*. New York: Mason Brothers, 1855.

Nathaniel Hawthorne, *Biographical Stories for Children*. Boston: Tappan and Dennet, 1842.

Nathaniel Hawthorne, *The Blithedale Romance*. Boston: Ticknor, Reed, and Fields, 1852.

Nathaniel Hawthorne, *Fanshawe: A Tale*. Boston: Marsh and Capen, 1828.

Nathaniel Hawthorne, *Grandfather's Chair*. Boston: E.P. Peabody; New York: Wiley and Putnam, 1841.

Nathaniel Hawthorne, *The House of the Seven Gables*. Boston: Ticknor, Reed, and Fields, 1851.

Nathaniel Hawthorne, *Life of Franklin Pierce*. Boston: Ticknor, Reed, and Fields, 1852.

Nathaniel Hawthorne, *The Marble Faun; or, The Romance of Monte Beni*. Boston: Ticknor and Fields, 1860.

Nathaniel Hawthorne, *Mosses from an Old Manse*. New York: Wiley and Putnam, 1846. Rev. ed., Boston: Ticknor and Fields, 1854.

Nathaniel Hawthorne, *Our Old Home*. Boston: Ticknor and Fields, 1863.

Nathaniel Hawthorne, *Peter Parley's Universal History*. Boston: American Stationers' Co., 1837.

Nathaniel Hawthorne, *The Snow-Image, and Other Twice-Told Tales*. Boston: Ticknor, Reed, and Fields, 1852.

Nathaniel Hawthorne, *Tanglewood Tales for Girls and Boys*. Boston: Ticknor, Reed, and Fields, 1853.

Nathaniel Hawthorne, *True Stories from History and Biography*. Boston: Ticknor, Reed, and Fields, 1851.

Nathaniel Hawthorne, *Twice-Told Tales*. Boston: American Stationers' Co., 1837. Expanded ed., Boston: James Munroe and Co., 1842.

Nathaniel Hawthorne, *A Wonder-Book for Girls and Boys*. Boston: Ticknor, Reed, and Fields, 1852.

Bibliography

Books

Joseph Alkana — *The Social Self: Hawthorne, Howells, William James, and Nineteenth-Century Psychology*. Lexington, KY: The University Press of Kentucky, 1997.

Barbara A. Bardes and Suzanne Gossett — *Declarations of Independence: Women and Political Power in Nineteenth-Century American Fiction*. New Brunswick, NJ: Rutgers University Press, 1990.

Sacvan Bercovitch — *The Office of "The Scarlet Letter."* Baltimore: Johns Hopkins University Press, 1991.

Nancy F. Cott — *The Bonds of Womanhood: "Woman's Sphere" in New England, 1780–1835*. New Haven: Yale University Press, 1977.

Frederick Crews — *The Sins of the Fathers: Hawthorne's Psychological Themes*. New York: Oxford University Press, 1966.

Paul John Eakin — *The New England Girl: Cultural Ideals in Hawthorne, Stowe, Howells, and James*. Athens: University of Georgia Press, 1976.

Susan Faludi — *Backlash: The Undeclared War Against American Women*. New York: Crown, 1991.

Barbara J. Harris — *Beyond Her Sphere: Women and Professions in American History*. Westport, CT: Greenwood Press, 1978.

Allan Lloyd Smith — *Eve Tempted: Writing and Sexuality in Hawthorne's Fiction*. Totowa, NJ: Barnes and Noble, 1984.

Thomas R. Mitchell — *Hawthorne's Fuller Mystery*. Amherst: University of Massachusetts Press, 1998.

Pam Morris — *Literature and Feminism: An Introduction*. Oxford: Blackwell, 1993.

Leland S. Person — *Aesthetic Headaches: Women and a Masculine Poetics in Poe, Melville, and Hawthorne*. Athens: University of Georgia Press, 1988.

Joel Pfister — *The Production of Personal Life: Class, Gender, and the Psychological in Hawthorne's Fiction*. Stanford, CA: Stanford University Press, 1991.

Susan Lynne Porter — *Women of the Commonwealth: Work, Family, and Social Change in Nineteenth-Century Massachusetts*. Amherst: University of Massachusetts Press, 1996.

Charles Swann — *Nathaniel Hawthorne: Tradition and Revolution*. Cambridge: Cambridge University Press, 1991.

Periodicals

Jonathan Arac	"The Politics of *The Scarlet Letter.*" In *Ideology and Classic American Literature*, edited by Sacvan Bercovitch and Myra Jehlen. Cambridge: Cambridge University Press, 1986.
Nina Auerbach	"The Rise of the Fallen Woman." *Nineteenth-Century Fiction* 35, no. 1 (June 1980): 29–52.
Phyllis W. Barrett	"More American Adams: Women Heroes in American Fiction." *Markham Review* 10 (Spring 1981): 39–41.
Nina Baym	"Portrayals of Women in American Literature, 1790–1870." In *What Manner of Woman*, edited by Marlene Springer. New York: New York University Press, 1977.
Nina Baym	"Thwarted Nature: Nathaniel Hawthorne as Feminist." In *American Novelists Revisited: Essays in Feminist Criticism*, edited by Fritz Fleischmann. Boston: G.K. Hall, 1982.
Carol Bensick	"His Folly, Her Weakness: Demystified Adultery in *The Scarlet Letter.*" In *New Essays on "The Scarlet Letter,"* edited by Michael J. Colacurcio. Cambridge: Cambridge University Press, 1985.
Morton Cronin	"Hawthorne on Romantic Love and the Status of Women." *PMLA* 69, no. 1 (March 1954).

Neal Frank Doubleday — "Hawthorne's Hester and Feminism." *PMLA* 54, no. 3 (September 1939).

Sylva Florence — "Studs vs. Sluts: The Eternal Double Standard." *The Penn* (Indiana, PA), November 18, 2002.

Rita K. Gollin — "'Again a Literary Man': Vocation and *The Scarlet Letter*." In *Critical Essays on Hawthorne's "The Scarlet Letter,"* edited by David B. Kesterson. Boston: G.K. Hall and Company, 1988.

Claudia Durst Johnson — "Impotence and Omnipotence in *The Scarlet Letter*." *New England Quarterly* 66, no. 4 (December 1993).

Paul K. Johnston — "Killing the Spirit: Anne Hutchinson and the Office of the Scarlet Letter." *Nathaniel Hawthorne Review* 22, no. 1 (Spring 1996).

David Leverenz — "Mrs. Hawthorne's Headache: Reading *The Scarlet Letter*." *Nineteenth-Century Fiction* 37, no. 4 (March 1983).

Michael J. Marks and R. Chris Fraley — "The Sexual Double Standard: Fact or Fiction?" *Sex Roles: A Journal of Research* 52, no. 3–4 (February 2005).

Robert Milder — "*The Scarlet Letter* and Its Discontents." *Nathaniel Hawthorne Review* 22 (Spring 1996).

Richard Millington
“The Office of *The Scarlet Letter*: An ‘Inside Narrative’?” *Nathaniel Hawthorne Review* 22, no. 1 (Spring 1996).

Krystian Moreno
“The Double Standards of Sex.” *Beacon* (Miami), March 7, 2005.

Ellen Sauerbrey
“Women Are Oppressed, Denied Opportunities in Too Many Places.” Address, 59th session of the UN Commission on Human Rights, Geneva, April 10, 2003. http://usinfo.state.gov/sa/Archive/2004/Jan/29-779774.html

Barbara Welter
“The Cult of True Womanhood, 1820–1860.” In *The American Family in Social-Historical Perspective*, 3rd ed., edited by Michael Gordon. New York: St. Martin's Press, 1983.

Index

D

E

F

G

H

I

Q

R

S

T

V

W

Y